CRITICAL A
SAFETY AND S
WOMEN WHO TRAVEL

"*Safety and Security for Women Who Travel* is packed with advice that can be applied to any destination, be it London or Lahore, including the process of getting in the right frame of mind for travel abroad."

—*Kansas City Star*

"It's an engaging little book, with plenty of first-person stories about strategies women have used while traveling to feel safe but still find their way into a culture."

—*Chicago Herald*

"In addition to their tips and wisdom, the authors offer memorable anecdotes that empower the most timid and most seasoned woman traveler."

—*Palo Alto Daily News*

"What's particularly good…is that it provides the necessary information without resorting to scare tactics."

—*Passport Book Review*

"*Safety and Security for Women Who Travel* offers ways to make traveling as comfortable, safe and enjoyable as possible."

—*Woman Newsmagazine*

"The book contains particularly useful tips on avoiding unwanted attention and choosing a traveling companion."

—*Traveler*

"…even the most seasoned traveler might learn something from *Safety & Security for Women Who Travel*."

—*Green Bay Press-Gazette*

"*Safety and Security for Women Who Travel*…is packed with worthwhile tips…"

—Barbara Hertenstein, *St. Louis Post-Dispatch*

TRAVELERS' TALES BOOKS

SAFETY AND SECURITY

FOR WOMEN WHO TRAVEL

SAFETY AND SECURITY

FOR WOMEN WHO TRAVEL

2nd EDITION

Sheila Swan and Peter Laufer

TRAVELERS' TALES
SAN FRANCISCO

Travelers' Tales and Travelers' Tales Guides are trademarks of
Travelers' Tales, Inc., 330 Townsend, Suite 208, San Francisco, California 94107.
www.travelerstales.com

Art direction by Stefan Gutermuth
Cover design by Stefan Gutermuth
Interior design by Susan Bailey and Kathryn Heflin
Page layout by Cynthia Lamb, using the fonts Berkeley, Copperplate, Savoye,
    and Birch

Distributed by Publishers Group West, 1700 Fourth Street, Berkeley, CA 94710.

Library of Congress Cataloging-in-Publication Data

Sheila Swan, 1942-
   Safety and security for women who travel / Sheila Swan and Peter Laufer. —2nd ed.
      p. cm. — (Travelers' Tales)
   Includes bibliographical references.
   ISBN 1-932361-15-4 (pbk.)
1. Women travelers. 2. Travel—Safety measures. I. Laufer, Peter. II. Title.
III. Travelers' Tales guides.
  G151.S93 2004
  910'.2'02082—dc22
                            2004018771

Second Edition
Printed in the United States of America
10 9 8 7 6 5 4 3 2 1

TABLE OF CONTENTS

PREFACE TO THE SECOND EDITION

The Cunard Lines' famous motto, "Getting there is half the fun," is no longer a guarantee after September 11, 2001. Nowadays, fun is the exception, especially with air travel, and getting there has become more of an ordeal. Many travelers fear getting there is dangerous, maybe even too dangerous to bother taking the trip. That's not true. Planning, knowledge, and awareness—combined with a little luck—is a recipe for a good journey.

I woke from a deep sleep that day. The phone was ringing. It was still early in California. On the line was a friend from Mexico.

"Sheila," he said, his voice sounded rattled. "Is Peter O.K.?"

"What are you talking about?" Peter was in Washington, D.C. on a business trip that week.

"Terrorists, Sheila, terrorists!" His voice was urgent. "Terrorists hijacked planes and dived them into New York and Washington. People are dead, killed by the planes crashing into...."

Of course I was shocked, but I was still half asleep, and my heart and sleepy head couldn't believe Milan was in his right mind. He insisted.

"Milan, I'll call you right back."

I ran upstairs to the answering machine. The message light

was blinking. I pushed play. "Sheila!" It was Peter's voice and I took a deep breath. "I want you to know that I'm O.K. The Pentagon was bombed. I can see it burning. I'll get in touch with you as soon as I can. All flights are cancelled. I love you."

I tried for hours to call him back on his cell phone. The circuits were jammed. I felt totally alone. Of course I didn't know if there would be more attacks. I was shocked and worried, along with the rest of America.

I easily could have been there with him. And during a crisis I think it's much worse being separated. We often travel together. Women or men, some issues are the same, such as basic survival.

The phone circuits were busy all day. When we finally spoke late that evening, Peter was stuck in Washington. No planes were flying. The trains were booked full. All the cars were rented.

Peter walked back to his hotel on the Virginia side of the Potomac, stopping at the first bank he could find and withdrawing the maximum he could get from the ATM. The mess on the streets in downtown Washington made it clear that American cities cannot be evacuated quickly in an emergency. The traffic was gridlocked for miles. By the time Peter arrived in Georgetown the National Guard was out in force, patrolling in their Humvees. He crossed the Key Bridge and looked downriver at the still-smoldering Pentagon.

Once back at the hotel, Peter started calling and recalling car rental companies. After a few days he finally secured a big, fast Buick and headed west.

We decided to meet in Reno. I would take a Greyhound there; we would spend the night somewhere in the desert and drive the last leg of his trip home to the coast together.

The country was still on edge, covered with God Bless America signs and waving flags. When my bus made its regular stop in Sacramento, I tried to find a sandwich and help a woman find the restroom. We were late getting back on and the driver was agitated.

"Hurry up!" he said, his voice gruff.

Back at my seat I noticed several men talking to passengers in a forced friendly manner. They seemed entirely too cheery, and they were asking extremely personal questions.

"Why are you traveling?" they asked one after another. "Where are you going?"

They skipped by me, and when they queried a young guy with dark hair on the other side of the bus I saw that they were flashing badges. But instead of feeling as if the authorities were making sure people were safe, it seemed to me more like an invasion of routine life. The Greyhound no longer felt like a safe zone.

A few days after we arrived home in California, commercial air traffic resumed. The flights were almost empty at first, and security was extreme and confused.

The next month we flew to Italy, determined not to allow the tragedy and its aftermath to curtail our lives on the road. The security line snaked through the airport lobby and doubled back on itself. It barely moved. When we finally reached the checkpoint I was pulled out of line for not removing my hat before I walked through the metal detector. A female guard was directed to take me to a search room. My purse and carry-on case came through the X-ray machine and sat on the counter while she took me away; she would not allow me to retrieve them. Peter gave me a high sign that he would grab them. Were I alone, they would have been out of my custody, free for the taking. She closed the door and had me take off the hat, gave me the all-body search, and apologized.

The crowds and confusion at the security gates are history now, replaced by federal agents of the Transportation Security Administration and ever increasing scrutiny of our documents and belongings. Of course post-9/11 security is not foolproof. There is always the human error factor at play, as a federal marshal made clear in early 2004 when she left her gun in the ladies room at Cleveland Hopkins International Airport. A passenger found the semiautomatic handgun and turned it over to an airport employee, who called police. The embarrassed marshal acknowledged that she put it on a shelf while she was washing her hands and promptly forgot all about it. "Obviously, we are very concerned," said her boss at the Air Marshal Service.

When going through airport security, no one asks me to take off my hat any longer, just my shoes since the metal in them sets off the alarm. A friend is stopped every time through because she wears a bra with a metal underwire. I've learned to travel without a corkscrew and without a nail file. Peter, who has no patience with guards pawing through his bags, never sets off the alarm anymore. His Swiss Army knife stays home in the dresser, and he carefully checks his pockets before he walks through the machine. We carry plastic sandwich bags for our coins and put them, along with glasses, pens, and cell phones, in our carry-ons. Our toothbrushes, combs, and other personal items are in plastic bags, too, so that if for some reason Homeland Security decides to search our bags, they can see what we're carrying and don't manhandle our toiletries with their dirty latex gloves.

But we still travel. By air and train, by boat and car. The

odds are with us and the thrill is worth the pain. The negative results of American foreign policy mandate we think twice before choosing some destinations since we carry U.S. passports, but over the years, and since 9/11, we've experienced over and over again the gratifying reality that most people the world over make a sophisticated differentiation between government and people. People everywhere love America and Americans, even while many of them reject our government's policies. They love American culture. They want to come to America. And they love meeting Americans and showing off their own countries.

INTRODUCTION

> Travellers sometimes buy jewels and bury them in their
> flesh. They make a gash, put the jewels in, and allow the flesh
> to grow over them as it would over a bullet. The operation is
> more to succeed if the jewels are put in a silver tube with rounded
> ends, for silver does not irritate. If the jewels are buried without
> the tube, they must have no sharp edges. The best place for
> burying them is in the left arm, at the spot chosen for vaccination.
> A traveller who was thus provided would always have a small
> capital to fall back upon, though robbed of everything he wore.
>
> —*Francis Galton,* Art of Travel *(1872)*

No woman needs go to such extremes today.

Las Vegas, winter. As usual, I was writing late at night while Peter dreamed; he writes in the morning while I sleep. The hotel was at the end of the strip, almost out of town—an adequate low-cost place. Outside the room, I sat in the corridor rewriting the notes I took during the day.

My bones were cold, sitting in the unheated hall. I kept my long purple wool coat on, a black angora beret on my head, and thick socks under my thin leather boots. With a drink from the bar, I was lost in my thoughts.

Security guards periodically walked back and forth, squawking on their walkie-talkies. This was Las Vegas—house security was in evidence even far from the famous casinos. I tried not to let them intrude on my work, but it was difficult, their radios were noisy.

"A woman," one of them said.

I continued to write.

Soon there were two security men huddled down the hallway.

"Send a female," I couldn't help but hear one of them request over his radio. Now I was a little interested in what trouble they were experiencing. A rowdy perhaps, down the hall, on the casino floor? I began to write down what was developing around me for some future story.

Suddenly the two guards and a woman surrounded me, hovering over me. The woman looked menacing and her voice was demanding.

"What are you doing here?"

"Writing," I said, looking now to see if they carry guns. "Why? What's wrong? What's going on here?"

"That's what we want to know," she barked back at me. "Are you a guest here?"

I said yes and began searching in my coat pocket for the key-card—just a strip of plastic with holes in it and no identifying hotel name or room number.

"What room are you in?" asked the demanding woman in a threatening voice. She, too, was in a hotel security guard's uniform.

"It's around the corner. I don't know the number."

"Don't move," she said. "What's your name?" The three of them stood over me like the guards they were.

"Sheila Swan," I said. "Sheila Swan Laufer. Look, whatever is wrong here, we can clear right up. I'll just go over to the room. My husband is in there."

"Don't move," was her response. One of the men was talking back and forth into his radio, saying my name. Irritation was combining with my surprise and initial confusion.

"I'm a guest in this hotel," I said. "Whatever is going on here is ridiculous...."

"We'll decide about that," the pushy woman interrupted me. "Stay put."

The guard talking on the radio looked up at the woman and reported, "No Lanfer here, no Swan."

"No, it's L-A-U-F like Frank E-R," I said. "Peter and Sheila. Just go around the corner, first door on the left. He will be asleep, but he will answer. Please." I'm not sure if it was the cold or the encounter, but I realized I was shivering, shaking.

"We don't disturb our guests."

"I'm a guest," I insisted. "Just go over there."

"Don't move."

I sat there thinking and watching them. What if the computer failed? No Laufer would come up on their screen. Would I be jailed for vagrancy or trespassing, or just thrown out of the hotel? At least if I were just thrown out I could call Peter from a pay phone. For the first time in my adult life I felt completely trapped.

Now years later, as Peter and I finish this safety and security guide for women travelers, that Las Vegas encounter came back to me vividly, as a reminder that—especially for women—trouble on the road can come in the most unexpected places and from those strangers you tend not to regard with suspicion. In these pages we deal with all sorts of threats women face on the road: from foreign customs and prejudices, to potential rapists and robbers, from specific health and hygiene needs to the vagaries of dating fellow travelers. And while awareness of risk is important, equally important is the attitude you bring to it, and your own honest assessment of yourself as a traveler—strengths and weaknesses, nightmares and desires, past experiences, and dreams for the future. Safety and security are affected by real outside circumstances, but they can also be powerfully affected by your state of mind.

We hope this book will help women travelers find an important delicate balance: enough consciousness about safety and security to help you get home healthy and happy without raising your anxiety level so that the journey becomes an exercise in paranoia and avoidance of those things that make travel so rewarding, the unexpected, the new, the serendipitous.

The Las Vegas guard's walkie-talkie squawked again with the message, "Yes. Laufer. Room 1221."

"Oh. Are you Mrs. Laufer?" asked my captor. "Can you please show us your key? We'll take you to your room."

"I don't need an escort." I was angry.

Nonetheless the three of them followed me as I walked to the room and pushed the strip of plastic into the door.

"You understand, Mrs. Laufer, it is for your security that we make sure everything is safe here in our hotel."

I shut the door, hard.

On the other hand, they were just doing their jobs, no malice intended; all the more reason for the experience to serve as a reminder to me of the tenuous nature of safety and security on the road.

A Bell Telephone System advertisement from the early 1950s quotes from a *Reader's Digest* story, "I was driving along a country road with four other women as my guests when a tire went flat. My heart sank with it, for my tire-changing experience was nil and the road was empty of aid. Pulling to the side, I hunted out the tools, remarking as I did so, 'Not a man in sight, of course. What we need is an angel from heaven!' Imagine our astonishment when a cheery voice from above our heads said, 'I'll be down in a minute, lady.' Unknowingly, I had stopped beside a telephone pole at the top of which sat our angel—a line repairman."

Of course even in the liberated twenty-first century most of us would still enjoy help with a flat tire, even if we're tattooed with Rosie the Riveter and "We Can Do It" on our biceps. Why not? But the world awaits us with and without help, and plenty of us enjoy traveling alone. This book is designed to help make your trips, as one of my best friends and I say to each other, filled with days of smooth sailing.

The advice in these pages offers specific and tested tactics and techniques to help you travel safely and securely. In all aspects of travel there is an element of danger and the information in this book will help you assess and reduce the risks to your own personal comfort level. However, there is no substitute—and never will be—for your own awareness and instinct supported by on-the-spot observation and information gleaned from locals.

Chapter One

BEFORE YOU LEAVE

The East looks to itself; it knows nothing of
the greater world of which you are a citizen,
asks nothing of you and of your civilization.

—*Gertrude Bell,* Safar Nameh-Persian Pictures *(1894)*

——————

Consider the case of a friend of mine who was carefully preparing for her first overseas trip to come and meet me in Paris. Hers was a well-planned trip, and during her research she read some horror story about European Gypsies targeting lone women to pickpocket. She bought a money belt, satisfied that her funds would be safe tight against her body.

When she told her husband and mother about her clever purchase, they teased her relentlessly.

"How are you going to feel safe getting out your money while pulling up your dress?" her husband laughed, for she never wore jeans or slacks, her wardrobe consisted only of dresses.

What works for one woman does not necessarily work for another. We must each make our own individual checklists to ensure that our own customs and habits are accommodated.

Preparation for a long-distance voyage does not eliminate the opportunity for discoveries and surprises on the road. Every trip is full of serendipity. Planning ahead leaves you free of many unnecessary burdens and allows you more freedom to simply enjoy yourself.

One evening in San Blas, Mexico I climbed a hill for a better vista of an outstanding sunset. By the time I returned to the car, mosquitoes had taken enough of my blood to help someone in need of a transfusion. My traveling companion actually counted them as I scratched all over—he stopped at ninety-five!

Had I packed some Benadryl, I would have at least enjoyed some relief through the night. (And the sandflies in New Zealand can make Mexican mosquitoes feel like a gentle tickling, but that's another story.)

I am not a methodical person in the rest of my life, but before a long trip, I rely on no one but myself.

First I go to my doctor for prescriptions for cough medicines and antibiotics, and other basic medicines which might not be easily available at my destination—just in case I get sick on the road. I fill my vitamin box, adding a spare bottle of Wellness Formula—a cold cure-all I believe helps knock out colds and flus when they first strike. Wellness Formula is concocted by a company called Source Naturals in Scotts Valley, California.

My doctor doesn't think it is necessary to be vaccinated against Hepatitis B, unless I travel deep into the outback of Third World countries. But I disagree and keep my Hep B shots current. I am not at any great risk since it's transmitted through blood and sex. I don't use needles and I'm married. But there are always the unknown possibilities: a needle stick, a sloppy

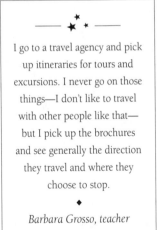

I go to a travel agency and pick up itineraries for tours and excursions. I never go on those things—I don't like to travel with other people like that—but I pick up the brochures and see generally the direction they travel and where they choose to stop.

♦

Barbara Grosso, teacher

kitchen worker. Although my health insurance doesn't cover the Hep B shots, I figure it's worth the investment. And it's not too expensive at my county health department clinic.

If you're a hiker or someone who just likes to walk through a field of wildflowers you may want to consider a vaccination for Lyme disease. Most insurance companies won't cover it either, and it's an expensive one, but then so are the treatments. If you can afford it, why not get it?

One week before my departure date, I check the weather at my destination—both in the daily newspapers, guidebooks, and the internet. Three days before I leave, my suitcase is packed with clothing that fits the climate. Two days before take-off, my carry-on bag is filled with all the things I'm convinced I cannot live without taking: extra contact lenses, my prescription for them, the stuff I use every night to wash my face. I leave this bag in my bathroom as I use the contents at home.

The day I leave, I simply place each of the things I use in my daily routine back in the bag as I get ready to go—toothbrush, toothpaste, hairbrush. This system ensures that none of my crucial daily tools are left behind.

And I aim for an afternoon flight, because I'm no morning person. Now that overseas flights require two-hour check-ins, I don't want to add to the stress of departure with worries that an early-morning rush might create some forgetfulness.

This is what I need to do to reduce the anxiety of preparing to leave home. Each person is of course unique in this way, but your goal is simply to be as tranquil as possible before you leave so that you arrive in better possession of your faculties.

You may already know a great deal about staying safe at home. Such experience and just good habits will serve you quite well abroad. But don't be surprised if you make mistakes and feel awkward as you adjust to new customs, languages, food, water, and time zones. Many travelers also experience loneliness and feelings of vulnerability that can come with being far away from home, family, and the familiar.

Tips

➤ Packing a destination-specific traveling medicine cabinet is well worth the trouble and expense. Most of the pills and sprays you'll want—the insect repellents and cramp relief compounds—that are available over the counter at home may be harder, if not impossible, to find once you get on the road. High-potency vitamin C, for example, the type available at any U.S. health food store or chain drug store, is an unknown item in many European stores, let alone Third World markets.

One of my cardinal travel rules: Invest in a pair of great walking shoes, and break them in before the trip. Comfortable feet mean less stress, less stress means I'm loose, light on my feet. I never wear thongs when I'm traveling—can't run in them.

◆

Margaret Bradford, photographer

➤ Ask your doctor to suggest and write prescriptions for medicines you may need specifically for the places where you are traveling. Get them filled at home, because the prescriptions may be invalid abroad. Keep the pills in their respective containers with the labels attached so that border guards don't suspect your vitamins or birth control pills to be illegal narcotics. (That's not as far-fetched as it sounds. Years ago Peter was held by the San Francisco police until he was able to convince them that what they claimed was peyote and LSD was, in fact, dried peaches and tapioca pudding mix!)

➤ A warm country can turn cold unpredictably. Bring clothes that can be layered easily to provide extra warmth. The lingerie sections of most department stores stock thin cotton tops that add protection without looking like bulky underwear.

➤ A long black dress and some dressy shoes should be packed in case of a chance meeting with a diplomat who invites you to a reception at the embassy or if you get an unexpected invitation to a symphony concert.

➤ Remember to do the standard pre-departure steps at your house like stopping the mail and the newspaper. Let a trusted neighbor know you're traveling. Leave a light on or buy a timer that turns a few lights on and off at irregular times to provide a lived-in appearance to the casual observer who may be casing your place. Consider arranging for the grass to be cut or the snow to be shoveled while you're gone.

➤ If you live alone, it might be worthwhile insurance to bring along a friend or someone with a dog when you do return home after a long time away, just in case somebody

> —— ★ ★ ——
>
> Dress down. Use really ratty backpacks, don't buy Gucci or high-end suitcases because those are the ones that people tend to target. Friends who traveled in South America took local feedbags and put them over their backpacks to not have Western backpacks visible on top of buses. Speaking a few words of the local language, even if you don't really know it, will throw people off. My brother would say always check in with the local embassy and make sure to give power of attorney to somebody in case something happens. Take copies of your passport with you and leave copies with someone at home, it makes replacement easier.
>
> ◆
>
> *Maria Hudnut, exporter*

uninvited is inside when you arrive. Leave a radio on tuned to a 24-hour news or talk station.

➤ Leave a key to your house with family members, trusted friends, or neighbors. You may need them to go in and check on something while you're gone. And, if you lose your own keys during the trip, you won't end up locked out of your own house.

Take earplugs. They create a sense of personal space. They abstract you from whatever is going on around you.

♦

Kay Ryan, poet

➤ Consider using a housesitter if you are going on an extended trip. Bad guys can tell if a house is not being lived in.

➤ Copy all your airline ticket numbers and airline phone numbers. Leave one with a friend at home and one copy packed separate from the tickets. If you lose your tickets or they are stolen, having those numbers and the itinerary will make it much easier to convince the airline to help you continue your journey.

➤ A photocopy of your credit cards and ATM cards will make on-the-road replacement much quicker and easier, and will make it faster for you to notify the companies if your cards are lost or stolen so that you will not be responsible for any fraudulent charges. On the reverse side of most cards is the company's emergency 800 number. 800 numbers can now be called from overseas for a standard toll charge.

➤ Passports, visas, and any requisite health certificates should also be photocopied and stored separately from the originals.

➤ If you want to reduce attention from strange men, wear a wedding ring and carry a photograph of your husband (or an ersatz husband) that you can show to persistent suitors. Another picture of the children at holiday time can be helpful too. Use anybody's children if you don't have a family.

Drink a lot of water before you fly and while you're in the air. You'll arrive in better shape, especially on a long trip.

♦

*Lynn Branden,
operations manager*

➤ You don't need to replace your suitcase with a cardboard box, or your camera case with a brown paper bag, but—depending on the potential dangers of your destination—you may wish to use ordinary-looking luggage that does not call attention to your relative affluence or your femininity.

➤ Use luggage tags that close over your name and address— hiding them from the view of would-be thieves and con artists.

➤ Make some effort to connect with women at home who have roots in the countries where you'll be traveling. You can find them easily at places such as ethnic restaurants, language schools, and social organizations.

➤ If a meal is being served on your flight, order a fruit plate or vegetarian plate at least 24 hours in advance, unless you like airplane food—or pack your own meal. Chances are you'll feel better on arrival.

➤ Expatriates living in America can provide contacts for you in their countries of origin and offer all sorts of ideas for your trips, from destinations the guidebooks may miss to places that it might be worthwhile for a woman to avoid. In addition, such a connection can help you learn what subtle customs and practices to expect, information that can make quite a difference for the woman traveler in many parts of the world.

➤ Bring a purse-sized flashlight and extra batteries for it. Hotels sometimes suffer power failures and you'll be happy to have your own light to see around the room and to help guide you out of the building.

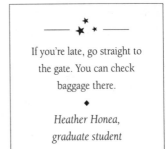

If you're late, go straight to the gate. You can check baggage there.

◆

Heather Honea,
graduate student

➤ It is vital for your security that you are not burdened by your luggage. Although it may seem convenient if some fellow offers to carry your bags, better not to allow it unless you know him or are certain he's an official baggage handler. Make sure you do not pack more than you can carry comfortably for long distances. Never be forced to compromise your safety because your belongings are too heavy or awkward to lug by yourself.

➤ Pack two cases, one with your vital necessities and the other with the types of clothing and incidentals that you can just abandon if you need to escape quickly from a dicey situation. You can always replace your clothes.

➤ Always carry with you those things that you really will be inconvenienced without: passport, credit cards, cash, and onward tickets. Never wander around without your passport. It is your ultimate identification to foreign authorities and if stolen, your passport is worth thousands of dollars on the black market. That can make it quite tempting to an underpaid hotel housekeeper or bell boy.

➤ Your purse should be a shoulder bag with a zippered closure. Always remember to close the zipper and hold on to the purse even if you wear it slung over one shoulder and across your body. Otherwise thieves in crowds can easily slash the strap and run with the purse or slit the purse itself and empty it of your wallet before you know you've been attacked. If you wear a fanny pack, avoid wearing it on your back where you can't see it.

➤ Bring along small unique presents to offer those who provide you with hospitality or assistance. If you work for a company that uses pens or pins or other tokens adorned with its logo for promotion, consider packing a handful of them. Similarly, simple tourist trinkets—even postcards—from your hometown will be well-received.

➤ To break the ice with children (and their parents), bring along a wind-up toy or simple game; if you play a small

---

Be honest with yourself is another major rule of travel. If you're fat and out of shape, don't try to climb a mountain. If you're afraid of water don't go on a raft trip. If you hate spiders and snakes, stay out of the tropics. If you can barely tolerate domestic flying, don't fly in Africa or South America, where some very funky things happen with air traffic. If you get a bad feeling about getting on that crowded bus or rusted prop plane, or you saw the pilot's red-rimmed eyes, don't get on board. Trust yourself. It's like a muscle that needs exercise.

◆

Stefania Payne, marathoner

instrument such as a harmonica, Jew's harp, or penny whistle, be sure to bring it and use it.

➤ Snapshots of your belongings as you pack them will help you deal with an insurance claim if your bags are lost or stolen.

I never take valuable jewelry with me. I never take anything exotic or expensive. I take real basic stuff, and I behave the way I behave at home: I avoid dark places late at night, lock my car, watch my purse. I don't really change my behavior. However, because I'm interested in getting to know people, I'm actually more open to meeting strangers when I travel than when I'm at home. You don't have to give away the store, you don't have to tell everything about yourself, you just size people up. So my guard is down a little bit more in terms of meeting people when I'm traveling but up in terms of all my material possessions and feelings of personal safety.

♦

Francine Keefer, journalist

Chapter Two

EN ROUTE

Good-bye. If you hear of my being stood up against a Mexican wall and shot to rags, please know that I think that a pretty good way to depart this life. It beats old age, disease, or falling down the cellar steps. To be a Gringo in Mexico—ah, that is euthanasia!

—*Ambrose Bierce, in a 1913 letter home*

——————

*N*o question I've been lucky in my travels. The worst physical assault I received was a slap on my legs from a crone in the main Mazatlan market. She was selling tiny chairs with woven seats and painted backs.

"You whore!" she spat at me in Spanish as she slapped me, "to walk around with your legs."

Nice-looking legs they were, at the time connected to a '60s California mentality that never considered a woman should cover them. I was lucky with that slap. Had I walked into a bar where the men viewed me as a whore, my blond self might have been in big trouble on that first trip to a foreign country.

That same afternoon I found a seamstress and some wonderful fabric. I paid her whatever she asked—I wasn't about to waste time bargaining—for four dresses that came down to my ankles. She sewed them on a treadle machine—all night, I imagine, because they were ready the next day.

In Morocco I bought a first-class train ticket for the ride from Casablanca to Marrakech figuring it would provide some comfort and space. It supplied neither. Six of us were jammed into the threadbare and smelly compartment, three on each side, elbow to elbow in the narrow seats, knees to knees. The most uncomfortable aspect of this journey was not the hot and smelly car or the body-to-body seating accommodations. It was the challenge of trying to avoid eye contact with the man sitting directly across from me. For hours and hours our knees were practically touching, but our eyes proved to be the biggest problem. Every time our eyes accidentally met, he looked embarrassed and upset, and he immediately looked away. I was bothered, too. I understood that in this Moslem environment it was inappropriate for us—strangers—to look at each other, but the seats were so close and the trip so long, it was extraordinarily difficult to prevent the periodic glance. I felt far away from the frivolity of the Crosby, Stills, Nash, and Young version of "Marrakech Express."

In most fundamentalist Islamic countries women are considered fast and loose if they walk around without being almost totally covered. In many countries that are predominantly Catholic, pants and an uncovered head are unacceptable for women inside a church. Even a handkerchief will suffice in an emergency for a head cover. In some cultures even looking a man in the eye is considered an invitation, and in many, traveling alone is evidence that you are in fact a whore or at least a woman of low morals.

When you land in another country, look around and see what the local women are wearing. They will be your key to appropriate dress and behavior. The best survival rule is to keep your body covered until you are certain that you will not cause yourself or others problems by exposing too much skin.

Your arrival in a foreign place can be an important transition time, whether you are there for the first time or a veteran of many visits. The more tranquil you can be as you face the challenge of a new culture, the more alert you likely will be not only to potential hazards, but to opportunities. One technique is to close your eyes as the aircraft is descending, breathe deeply, and imagine yourself smiling as you encounter crowds of people, the babel of languages. Your life is about to change, as it always does on a journey. Consider avoiding the mad rush to the exit of the aircraft, and if you are seated toward the rear of the plane, take the time instead to rest, to compose yourself for the important moments ahead.

On one long intercontinental flight, I was lucky to sit next to a delightful Irish woman from Dublin. Fiona and I started talking when we were ordering dinner and after ordering the same meal and the same wine, we kept chatting, realizing we had plenty in common. We talked about our mutual love for travel, and I told her I thought she was lucky, since she was able to travel the world on a European passport at a time when the familiar gold eagle on the blue U.S. passport could be considered a target.

Fiona smiled, reached for her green Irish passport and pulled off the leather cover.

"Here," she said. "I just bought this. I can get another."

She handed me the cover, which fits nicely over my own passport. *An Comhphobal Eorpach*, it says in Irish, European Community. Over the gold outline of the island are the words *Éire* and Ireland.

I enjoy looking at the new cover of my passport. It reminds me of my fleeting friendship with Fiona, and I'm not so conspicuously American when I'm standing in lines with my passport ready to show guards and officials. I like not being conspicuously American, not only because of the contemporary political problems in the world, but also because my casual encounters with others are not prejudged if they do not know for certain my origin.

At the Mexico City airport I always choose the higher priced taxi ride to my hotel. The yellow-and-white cabs with the silhouette of an airplane on the door are the most expensive cab ride downtown. You can flag down one of the cheap old green VW bugs, but the drivers are not forced to pass the more arduous licensing requirements faced by the airport-authorized taxis. Their cars are rickety, and the price is negotiated curbside. The bigger and newer airport cabs operate with a fixed rate.

On one memorable trip, all the luggage was in the cab and we were on our way while I was still fumbling for the seat belts, reaching around groping until it was clear there were none. We were already out in the traffic and I just shrugged, *Qué será, será.* I was raised without seat belts and survived just fine. This may have been due to my father's automatic arm that shot out across my chest if he thought there was some sort of danger. I sat back watching the rush-hour traffic jammed on the highway as we struggled toward the *zócolo,* maybe going twenty-five miles per hour. The driver had said it might take us an hour. An hour would have been great.

Without warning the taxi was smashed into on the left rear side. I held on, bracing my legs as the car spun across three lanes of traffic, hit the center guard rail and careened back across those same lanes. *Gracias a Dios,* it was a miracle no one was hurt, including the guy whose now-wrecked car was planted behind us. He apologized to all several times. I was dazed. The driver was speaking on his radio, reporting the accident and asking for another taxi. I asked him to request one that was equipped with seat belts.

Later I was pleased to determine that the only thing wrong with me was sore legs from bracing myself, a protective action that kicked in automatically.

Since that day, whenever possible, I never get into a taxi

without first checking out the seat belts, and I feel quite comfortable saying a polite, "No thanks. No seat belts, no ride."

Tips

➤ While waiting in line to go through passport control, don't hold your passport out in front of you with the easily recognizable American eagle shining out at every opportunistic man seeking an opening. Hold it against your immigration and customs papers with the eagle and "United States of America" side hidden. There is no need to advertise your citizenship to fellow travelers, some of whom may harbor deep prejudices against the U.S. or strange ideas about American women and see you as a potential target.

➤ Choose your traveling garb carefully—not too revealing, unless you want to court random romantic attention. Make sure it's comfortable for long flights and easy to release in cramped airplane toilet facilities. Shun logo t-shirts and other markings that make it easy for hustlers to make an approach that can catch you off guard. Just as parents are warned not to send their kids around town with their names plastered all over their clothing, you'll find it easier to be in charge of encounters with strangers if they aren't starting conversations with you based on the football team or saloon advertised on your shirt.

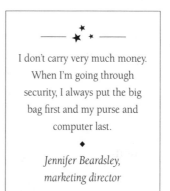

I don't carry very much money. When I'm going through security, I always put the big bag first and my purse and computer last.

♦

Jennifer Beardsley,
marketing director

➤ At the airport and at borders, seek out other women (particularly Western tourists) coming out of the country you're headed for. Ask them for advice. Most women are happy to share information and knowledge, and these women are ideal primary sources. They can tell you from first-hand experience what worked for them and what you might need to worry about and avoid. They can offer up-to-the-minute tips on restaurants and night clubs. They may even have some names and addresses to share.

> I try to give myself plenty of time so I'm never in a rush, arriving or leaving. I also plan my schedule so I'm not forced to eat in the hotel restaurant and spend a small fortune because I'm afraid to walk outside.
>
> ◆
>
> *Liz Duffy, cataloguer*

➤ Remember the buddy system. Even if you are traveling alone, you'll find opportunities to meet temporary buddies. Conversations with seatmates on a long plane ride can provide you with enough of a rapport and enough confidence to suggest sharing a cab from the airport, and other casual joint ventures. The stress of the initial entry into a foreign port can be eased with a companion.

➤ When possible, don't stash your luggage in the cab trunk in case you need to quickly leave the taxi.

➤ If your seatmate takes advantage of the close proximity of airplane seating to touch you inappropriately, tell the flight attendants immediately. They will find you an alternative place on the plane. Choosing an aisle seat puts you in a much easier position to leave an uncomfortable or threatening situation.

➤ Do not hesitate to inform the flight attendants if you feel ill in the air. Most commercial airplanes are now equipped with defibrillators, the device that can save lives with a shock to the heart. First aid kits have been upgraded in recent years to treat much more serious complaints than cuts and bruises. Flight crews are quick to request help from doctors and nurses who may be on board. They are in radio contact with doctors on the ground for consultation, and if the issue is acute they may decide to make an emergency landing.

➤ Tear your name and address off any magazines you bring from home to read en route.

➤ To reduce swelling ankles, wear shoes on the plane that slip off easily, and bring a sweater on the flight to compensate for the airplane air conditioning—sometimes brutally cold even during flights from one hot climate to another. Carry at least one pair of comfortable walking shoes and don't bother bringing along new shoes that are not broken in already.

> I always bring material to read, since airplanes are so often delayed. When I travel, I try to take some common medicines, like allergy pills or Tylenol, rather than think that I can get it at the next stop. It's better to be prepared.
>
> ◆
>
> *Vicky Su, accountant and business owner*

➤ Take the time to learn just a few words in the local

language. Even if you have no talent for languages, being able to say things like *hello, please, thank you, no, I have a disease, I am sick, I need a doctor, call the police,* and *I need help,* can be crucial. If you really can't remember them, write them phonetically on a card and keep the card with you.

➤ Other words that are important to understand are those that may be said to you, or may be on signs, and could cause you distinct trouble if they are ignored. *Stop, no, forbidden, danger* and *no photographs* are vital to know.

➤ You may well feel disoriented at the beginning of a trip— the new territory, the jet-lag, the change in routine. Try not to make critical decisions during the first few days of travel.

➤ If your luggage is lost, report it to the airline before you leave the airport. Much lost luggage just missed the flight and shows up on the next one. Usually the airline will send it to your hotel as soon as it arrives for no charge. Sometimes first class and tourist baggage comes in on different carousels, so look at the carousels used for first class passengers' baggage even if you travel economy. Before you file a lost luggage form, check all carousels from your plane. A distinguishing mark on your suitcase, such as a piece of yarn or sticker that means something to you, makes it much easier to locate on the baggage carousel.

When I'm traveling with my children, I enforce a "no sweets" rule. Everyone stays calmer that way, and we all arrive a little less frazzled.

◆

Larissa Mendez, mechanic

➤ If a genuine emergency occurs and you must return home immediately, many airlines will go out of their way to accommodate you no matter how restrictive your ticket.

➤ To avoid the vulnerable look of a woman standing around in the airport or the main square, guidebook in hand, searching for a hotel, book at least your first night's room in advance. It may cost more than you need or want to pay, but it is worth the security of knowing you'll be off the streets while you adjust your senses to being away from familiar home territory. If you book directly with the hotel instead of using a reservation service or a travel agent, you may get a discount that will more than pay for the long distance phone call. Always get the name of the clerk you speak with and a reservation number so that if there is a question about your accommodation when you arrive, you have a contact. And always ask to see the room before you take it. Some nice-looking lobbies are the front for dreadful little rooms.

I roll most of my clothes up so they don't get wrinkled, and I put in enough underwear and socks in case I have to stay over a few extra days.

♦

Margaret Chaika, pulmonary rehabilitation coordinator

➤ Consider packing a product called a travel sheet or sleep sack. It is an easily packed cotton or silk bag to sleep in on the chance that you end up in a hotel with sheets that don't meet your standards for cleanliness. You can also use it as an easily-washed liner for sleeping bags.

➤ When you reach your accommodations, put a hotel business card into your pocket and purse. If you're out and about and a language barrier exists, showing the card to a police officer or a cab driver will make your return easier.

➤ Do your best not to get lost. Not knowing where you are in a strange land can put you in an extremely vulnerable position. Make mental notes of landmarks as you leave your hotel. If you have a poor memory jot notes down on a notepad or trace your route on a compact city map that is small enough so that it does not draw attention to your being an out-of-towner. You should always endeavor to feel secure in your ability to retrace your steps.

➤ If you do become disoriented regarding your whereabouts, check with a shopkeeper or a police officer for directions—not a stranger on the street—unless you want to take advantage of being lost to get into a conversation

I keep my stuff with me, even when I go into the bathroom.

♦

Joan Wallner,
recreation coordinator

and a relationship with the stranger. Even if you *are* lost, don't *look* lost. Carry yourself as if you know what you are doing and where you are going.

➤ When you enter a country, find out if you need an exit visa or if there is an exit tax for departure and if it must be paid in local currency. If there is an exit tax, set aside the amount you'll need right at the start of your trip. If you are unprepared for these requirements, the delay obtaining them can cause you to miss a connection.

➤ Earplugs can be a godsend to the traveler struggling with jet lag, especially if you are a light sleeper, or staying in a place where there are barking dogs, construction, or thin walls.

When I arrive at a new place, I always look around once quickly to check out the scene. I look for things that seem wrong or out of place, for people who make me uneasy. Then I trust my intuition — and move on if I'm not comfortable.

♦

Lorna Hanhy, artist

Chapter Three

MONEY AND SCAMS

We landed here in March. I wait tables
to make money. I can do this and
sail all around the world.

—*Waitress in a South Seas restaurant (1998)*

⸻

ew things are more crucial for a woman's safety and security on the road than money and access to money. It is much more difficult to operate independently if you are burdened by doubts about the reliability of your cash flow. Not too long ago, this was much more of a problem than it is these days. Travelers' checks were the only viable alternative to carrying cash and getting money wired from home was an expensive and complicated procedure.

Today it is a rare and isolated outpost that is without an ATM. Most major U.S. banks are connected with overseas partners through cooperative networks such as Cirrus, the Star System, and Global Access (yours are listed on the reverse side of your ATM card). Your local bank can check to make sure your ATM card will deliver cash in the country you are visiting, and what the bank will levy for a service charge.

However, the technology can fail you. As credit cards rub against each other in your wallet, the magnetic strip on the back becomes worn and eventually will not trigger a valid response from ATMs. Foreign banks will *not* authorize a manual cash withdrawal for you even if you have your ATM card and offer to disclose your password. A card that won't work in the machine is worthless for providing you with needed cash *unless* it is a dual system card that can be used as either a debit card or a Visa or MasterCard credit card. Foreign banks will accept such dual cards and provide you with a cash advance based on the credit information on the face of the card.

If your ATM card is not also a credit card, ask your bank to issue you one of the dual cards. If they refuse because your credit history is inadequate for their restrictions, make sure you travel with a regular Visa or MasterCard, or some other credit card that you are sure will enable you to charge a cash advance. Remember that these cash advances carry enormous interest rates unless you pay them back during the first billing cycle. Although such cash advance transactions can be costly, they can be lifesavers.

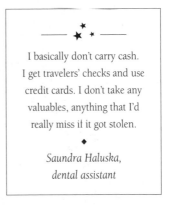

I basically don't carry cash. I get travelers' checks and use credit cards. I don't take any valuables, anything that I'd really miss if it got stolen.

◆

Saundra Haluska,
dental assistant

In rural areas or developing countries where ATMs may be a rare find, exchange some cash as soon as you arrive at the border or the airport to keep you solvent until you find the banks with the best rates.

When you travel to poor countries or regions, you should be aware that in the eyes of most of the natives, you are a very rich person, even if you spent your last dime setting up your trip. For many, the very possession of a U.S. passport marks you as wealthy—you come from the promised land as seen around the world in movies and American TV shows. When you are traveling in more developed countries, it is just as important to remember that your profile as a tourist or foreigner can mark you as an appealing target for scam artists and thieves.

Most Americans have not grown up in a thriving street market culture, and many novice travelers have a difficult time bargaining or understanding the psychological, emotional, and cultural currents at work with foreign merchants. If, on the other hand, you think of yourself as a savvy haggler or bargainer, it is wise to recall Rudyard Kipling's famous line: "Here lies a fool who tried to hustle the East." Chances are, the good deal you think you got also left a big smile on the merchant's face, an ideal circumstance. Enjoy the challenge of haggling in street markets, but don't expect to outsmart the locals. Try to find out if there are any special rules of the game you should be aware of, especially what actions on your part might signify serious interest you might prefer to keep to yourself.

Con artists and sexual predators can be a problem both at home and in foreign countries. The main difference lies in your heightened vulnerability when you are abroad. You may be hesitant to offend, feeling that you are misjudging cultural differences or language nuances, and therefore be hesitant to rebuff people even when your personal warning bells are ringing. Remember, the dangerous con artist can move quickly from someone who is merely trying to part you from your belongings to someone who may seriously harm you.

There are techniques to help you turn up the volume on your inner warning bells. The best defense is to have a roadmap of some of the more obvious tactics predators worldwide use. Gavin de Becker notes seven tactics in his book *The Gift of Fear* that apply not only to sexual predators, but also to con artists of all types in all cultures. There are simple stratagems that can help a predator to invade your personal space, create unsolicited links, maneuver you with charm, distract you with too many irrelevant details, manipulate you, create indebtedness where none exists, and basically help an intruder refuse to take no for an answer.

All scams, sexual and otherwise, attempt to shift control from you to the con artist. A recognition of these tactics can make an enormous difference in how you choose to respond. Let's say you're claiming your baggage in an airport and a man who has overheard your conversation comes up to you and says, "I can tell from your accent that you're from Minnesota, so am I! We Minnesotans need to stick together, let me help you with your bags." This might be a perfectly innocent offer of help from a nice man, but it may just as easily be an attempt to create a familiarity that does not in fact exist, in order to get you to let your guard down long enough for him to steal your bags or hustle you for sexual favors, or both. Be wary of people who take advantage of information gleaned from things you wear (like clothing with a logo or message) and your luggage. Watch out for people who use your first name too often or too soon.

In short, pay attention to any warning signal that intuition or common sense tells you is inappropriate.

Tips

> Guard your PIN carefully, whether it be your ATM PIN or your telephone credit card number. Stand close when you punch it in at a pay phone. Phone card thieves work public places with binoculars. Peter's PIN was spotted by a thief at Kennedy Airport who ran up hundreds of dollars in calls to Ireland. If this happens to you, the phone company will clear the charges off your bill if you can make a good case that they break your normal calling pattern.

➤ Check the expiration dates so that your credit cards (and your passport!) do not expire while you are traveling. Make sure you get your own card back when you hand it to a clerk. Check with your credit card companies about what additional services they offer, such as travel insurance and guarantees for merchandise.

➤ It's easy to feel safe and comfortable on a plane, but if you leave your seat and you're traveling alone, take your bag with your onward tickets, money, and passport with you. You may feel secure enough leaving your things with a seatmate you've been talking with for hours and with whom you have established some rapport. Let your intuition guide you, of course.

➤ Know the currency. Take along a pocket-sized calculator to figure the various exchange rates you encounter. If you're moving from place to place and rate to rate, the conversion can become confusing and a mistake can cost you plenty. Consider making a chart that

In Bangkok, it's fun to ride *tuk-tuks*, the little motorized rickshaws you see buzzing around all over the place. But be careful, sometimes the drivers are in cahoots with merchants such as tailors and jewelers. So instead of getting to your destination, first you are pressured to visit an establishment or showroom on the way. Refuse, make a stink.

◆

Margaret Bradford,
photographer

I put my cash in my pocket, instead of in a wallet. I basically strip my purse, I have one charge card, that's it. So if my purse gets stolen, I'm not financially crippled.

◆

Chris Minner,
wife and mother

you can glance at so that you can get an immediate idea of what something costs in U.S. dollars. Do not allow a shopkeeper to pressure you into a fast transaction. The foreign currency values initially might be confusing and you can lose a lot of money if you don't take the time and effort to know what things are really costing.

➤ Stash your U.S. money and your foreign money in two different places in your purse so that when you reach for the local money no one sees a stack of valuable and attractive U.S. bills. The separation also makes it easier for you to differentiate between the values of the two currencies. Keep small amounts of money for incidental purchases separate from your main supply so that you do not need to expose your billfold when you're buying small items.

> Cabbies are often the first scam artists you have to deal with on arrival. The basic scam is taking the long route to anywhere. So it might be wise to take a little map with you and figure out where you're supposed to go. Cabbies also offer to help you find a hotel and if there's some sort of kickback involved, it might not be the best choice of hotel for you. They know you're brand new in the country. They're picking up virgins at the airport.

◆

Fay Faron,
private detective

➤ Whenever possible change your money by withdrawing it from an ATM. You'll get a better rate than with travelers' checks or cash, and it's convenient. Watch your back at the machine, just as you would at home. But remember that each withdrawal carries a service charge. Most international airports and train stations are equipped with ATMs. Change enough on arrival to get you through the first night. You don't need the anxiety of looking for an ATM in addition to the stress and excitement of arrival in a new locale.

➤ If you can afford it, keep at least a hundred dollars of American cash with you for emergencies. U.S. money is still one of the most popular currencies in the world and if you run out of the local currency, you'll be able to handle emergencies even if the exchange rate is unfavorable for you. Carry fifty or twenty dollar bills. Since the U.S. hundred dollar bill was redesigned, it no longer is as universally appreciated and accepted as it once was. In addition, keep a few one and five dollar bills with you, especially in developing countries. They make appreciated tips.

> ——— ⋆⋆ ⋆ ———
>
> My main key is keeping things as close to my body as possible. I carry a very tiny purse that can hold only a wallet and an aspirin case. I can wear it under my coat and I can wear it inside a dress. I bring it around to the front of me. If I am going to carry my wallet in a pocket, I make sure it is a deep pocket in front of me.
>
> ◆
>
> *Lynn Hassan, artist*

➤ During electrical blackouts and telephone breakdowns, credit card machines fail to function. That means a hotel or restaurant may refuse to accept anything but cash. Your hundred dollar bill may keep you fed and lodged. If you feel a natural or manmade disaster is imminent, consider withdrawing the maximum cash possible from the closest ATM. Not only is it likely that ATMs will fail to function during some crises, but they could well run out of cash quickly. During emergencies, cash can be crucial.

➤ No matter how tempting it may be, avoid the black currency market. Saving a few dollars (or even more) by changing money illegally is not worth the risk for at least two important reasons. One is that you could end up in a dangerous foreign prison for years. (Read Peter's book *Nightmare Abroad* if you want a picture of how grim this can be!) Another is that you could be swindled by a cheating money changer. In many of the countries where a black market deal would be alluring, the currency is unstable and frequently devalued. That often means bank notes with high numbers are retired out of circulation, replaced with newly designed bills that have fewer zeros. Unscrupulous money changers sell unsuspecting travelers old—and worthless— currency that looks just like the real thing, because it once was. Sometimes it's counterfeit. Some even sell the much less valuable currency of an adjoining country to tourists who cannot read the local languages and only look at the numbers on the bills.

➢ When you go out, always carry enough cash for at least one direction of bus or cab fare and enough to make a phone call. It is also wise to carry a pre-paid phone card.

➢ Take your sweet time counting your change from cab drivers, whether you're in Paris or Phnom Penh. You're at the mercy of cab drivers when you're flustered by language, holding up traffic, and the driver has added on all sorts of special charges

---
★ ★
★ ★ *

In Jamaica, I got to the airport and the taxi driver came up in a very aggressive manner, and even after all my traveling, I was still naive I suppose because I got in his cab. He took me all over Kingston, through the neighborhoods, and ran up quite a bill. I'm very careful now to check with the official dispatchers in the airport.

◆

Karen Sandel,
international consultant

beyond what's on the meter. Some of the worst offenders are in Paris and Rome; among the best and most honest are those in London.

➤ Keep track of what you charge to your room so that you can check it against your bill. Mistakes are made. Perhaps the hotel staff may be arrogant regarding requests to amend your bill. In that case, be polite and persistent. Don't hesitate to ask for the manager.

➤ If you are traveling far from the world's major capital cities, consider the value of an American Express card. American Express now offers credit cards that do not carry an annual fee. These cards will provide you with access to American Express offices worldwide, where you can receive forwarded mail. If you run out of funds, transfers to American Express offices are simple to conduct.

⭐ ✶

I don't put my wallet or anything of real value in a day pack. I keep my keys in a pocket that's on my body, not in an outer jacket pocket. I want them in my skirt or in my pants and I make sure my pocket is deep enough so that they won't fall out when I sit down. One of the things my sister has done is to sew big, deep additional pockets in pants.

◆

Lynn Hassan, artist

Chapter Four

DRIVING

The street was very much thronged, and I thought the crowd a more
civil and orderly one, than an English crowd. The men did not jostle
or push one another, or tread upon one's feet, or kick down one's
shoe heels, or crush one's bonnet into one's face, or turn it around
on one's head, all of which I have seen done in London streets.

—*Fanny Kemble,* Journal *(1835)*

omen can look like particularly easy targets to carjackers and smash-and-run thugs. Even with a man
in the car. Peter's mother was traveling in Italy with
his sister and her husband (and their children) when she
refused to become a victim.

Vesuvius was in back of them, the blue Mediterranean to
the left. Of course the car doors of the Volvo were locked. The
windows were up, too. They were on the main waterside road
going north towards Naples, still not quite in the city itself, just
in an ugly industrial sprawl. They stopped at a red light.

Peter's mother was in the front seat; his brother-in-law was
driving. Suddenly a guy on a motor scooter pulled up to his
mother's window, and smashed it with a huge drill bit (his
sister kept it for a souvenir). Glass shattered everywhere,
including all over his mother.

Then the robber put what Peter's sister describes as "his big
fat hairy muscley arm" through the space where the window
had been and grabbed her purse. He didn't know Peter's
mother. She held on to it and held on tightly. His brother-in-

law started hitting the invading arm from the driver's side and Peter's sister screamed loudly and relentlessly.

After what seemed like a couple of minutes to them in the car, the potential robber pulled his arm out as the light changed and they drove to a fancy hotel where, as his sister remembers, "Everyone apologized in the name of all Italy and the Pope, and gave us coffee."

They filed a police report, but of course the thief was never found, and the window was repaired.

Despite the happy ending, in retrospect Peter's sister has second thoughts about their actions. "Tell your readers that we did the wrong thing," she says. "If we had thought first then we would have stepped hard on the gas immediately."

You may not wish to run a red light into oncoming traffic, but it might be a better alternative than standing still at the mercy of an assailant.

Of course, to do what Peter's sister was suggesting, you have to know whether you can, in self-defense, cause serious bodily harm to another.

A study commissioned by the Automobile Association in England found that up to 70 percent of women worry about their personal security and safety when they are behind the wheel. Among the tactics used by women in an attempt to reduce their odds of encountering trouble, according to the AA researchers: avoiding unfamiliar roads and roads they fear will be deserted—especially at night—and dressing like men while driving alone.

After a long cold bus ride to Agadir (none of the passengers complained, old women were bundled up in blankets), Peter needed to go back to the States, and I considered Agadir might be a relaxing place for me to wait in Morocco until he returned. But it turned out to be a desolate tourist-filled resort, wrecked by an earthquake and poorly rebuilt with sixties-style concrete hotel and apartment blocks. I thought it seemed a far better thing to go up the coast to Essaouira, the site of Jimi Hendrix's "Castles in the Sand," a fishing port with an intact medina, a place an old friend of ours told great tales about from his days living there in the 1970s.

I rented a car from the Africar agency, waiting with our son while Mohammed retrieved it from the lot and cleaned it. We ate some ice cream and visited a store that sold trinkets to tourists. Michael felt so sorry for the endless number of skinny cats roaming the sidewalks that we bought some cat food. He was amazed that none of them wanted it. Obviously the store stocked cans of cat food for the expatriates who brought their cats with them, cats accustomed to the commercial feed. Local cats ate local leftovers.

Mohammed finally came with the car and as I was about to get into it for the long drive north I noticed a stink of gasoline. I looked under the car; gas was leaking all over the parking lot.

"Mohammed," I pointed to the pool growing under the car, "this is not acceptable."

"No problem, ma'am," he smiled. "I'll fix that right away."

Half an hour later three guys were still working on the problem. Finally I told Mohammed that I was not going to take the leaking car, and asked him to please find another one. He pulled out his cell phone, made some calls trying to round up a different car, still insisting the leak would be fixed soon. Soon meant nothing there. I was adamant. I needed a different car. I did not trust the repair job and I was rapidly losing the day. I didn't want to spend another night in Agadir. Soon I would be forced to drive on dark roads I didn't know, something that's rarely a good idea.

Mohammed produced a different car. We managed to arrive

in Essaouira before dark, but not before it began to rain (the windshield wipers didn't work, neither did the heater). But it was a great ride up the coast. We saw Morocco's famous goats that climb up trees to forage, eating nuts that pass through their systems and then are harvested by Moroccans who make them into a cooking oil considered gourmet. Roadside stands offered the oil, waving merchants coaxing us to buy it as we rode right by.

Essaouira turned out to be the dream of a town we expected, a far better place than Agadir. Stand your ground when you're renting a car. Make sure you're happy with it. Carefully check it out to make sure everything works properly. I should have checked the wipers, but I was so glad to get the replacement car with no gas leak I just wanted to get on the road.

Africar was inexpensive; Mohammed was gracious. The problems wouldn't keep me from renting from him again. But my hand ached by the time we arrived in Essaouira from operating the wipers manually.

Tips

➤ Most experts agree the safest thing to do when faced with a purse snatcher is to let go and leave. If you keep a photocopy of your passport in a separate place from your purse, the closest American consulate can replace it for you in a few hours.

➤ Lock the car doors whenever you leave the car, no matter how safe the situation looks. With the power locks that most rental cars come equipped with, you can lock the doors without drawing attention to your action. It is always more difficult to get someone out of your car once they're in than to keep them out to begin with.

➤ For the same reason, lock the doors when you are in the car and while you're driving. This way, you're in a better position to decide who gets in the car with you. Unfortunately, carjackings occur and women can look like vulnerable victims. Simply keeping the car door locked can prevent the casual car jacker and thief from getting into your car.

➤ Gas up when the tank is half empty to avoid running out of gas or to keep from being forced to look for gas in neighborhoods you might otherwise avoid, especially as a woman alone. In some countries, 24-hour gas stations are unknown. Try to fill up the tank before you go to sleep at night so that if you need to put miles between you and whatever or whomever you want to get away from during the

---

A woman I know was rescued by a cab driver. She was being hassled on the street and he escorted her into his taxi. But the guy who was hassling her came after her inside the car. The cab driver screamed at him and gunned the car in his direction. Later my friend wondered if he really would have run the other guy down. I guess you never know about something like that until it happens.

◆

Anonymous

I lock the doors when I'm driving and I'm aware of my surroundings. I'm not paranoid, but I check to make sure no one is following me. I don't drive with my windows down, even in the summertime, because of carjacking. At night I park close to where I'm going, and always in a lighted place.

◆

Lorna Hanhy, artist

night or in the morning, you
need not worry about fuel.

For me, a day on the road is no
different than a day in life.
Plainly because it is life.

♦

Laurel Hirsch, writer

➤ Much of the world drives on
the left-hand side of the
road: the British, their former colonies from India and
Hong Kong to Australia and
New Zealand, along with Japan and Ireland. If you are
going to rent a car and drive on the left, do not expect to
just jump in the car and take off on a marathon ride the
first day. It takes at least a few days or more of extra-careful
driving to get used to the opposite side of the street and to
looking right first at intersections, instead of left. Renting a
car with an automatic transmission will make the transition
easier, although cars equipped with an automatic may well
cost more to rent.

➤ The same cautionary note goes for being a pedestrian in
these places.

➤ If you are traveling with children, whether they are toddlers
or teens, be especially careful to show them—and remind
them daily—how the traffic moves differently. It is all too
easy to forget, with potentially disastrous results.

➤ If you are shipping your own car to a left-side driving
country, or taking a British-style right-hand drive car
to the Continent or other places where the driving is on the
right side of the road, expect even more trouble. It is extraordinarily disorienting to be on a strange side
of the road and drive from the wrong side of the car.
Distances are difficult to judge, passing on a two-lane road
is excruciating—you must get your car into the oncoming

traffic lane before you can see if any traffic is headed at you. Allow at least two days to get used to that phenomenon before you take off on a long drive.

➤ Lower your tourist profile at gas and food stops by keeping guidebooks and maps hidden under a local newspaper. There is no need to advertise that you're just passing through. A paper book cover can be made out of a local newspaper (the type we used on high school textbooks) for guidebooks. Camouflaging the guidebook is an easy device to help set the ground rules for interaction with the locals. They don't need to know as soon as they set eyes on you that you're a tourist. But don't be furtive when you look at your guidebook and risk attracting unwanted attention with your self-consciousness.

> ─── ★ ★ ────
>
> I rented a car from Hertz in Japan, planning to drive from Hokkaido through the countryside to the northernmost village of Japan, Wakkanai. As I left the airport, I realized I simply could not read any of the road signs. I immediately was getting lost, stymied by my inability to read Japanese. I returned the car to Hertz and took the train to Wakkanai.
>
> ◆
>
> *Anonymous*

➤ Check rental cars for signs that identify them as rentals. Since a rash of tourist shootings in Miami, the state of Florida no longer uses special—and easily identifiable—license plates for rented cars. Some car rental companies still adorn their cars with bumper stickers to advertise their services. Pull them off. You do not need to yell, "I'm not from around here!" as you drive through strange neighborhoods.

➢ There are thousands of highway crimes in the United States. Rest stops at night are particularly dangerous for single women. A cellular phone that is both visible and within easy reach is a good crime deterrent.

➢ Carjackers often operate in pairs. They are often armed and approach from both sides of the car when you are parked or stopped. Your best chance of survival (assuming you can't escape with the car) is to hand over the car immediately, and run.

➢ Don't be coerced by clerks at the rent-a-car counters who try to sell you insurance. If you rent with a gold-faced Visa or MasterCard, you may well be covered completely. Before you go, check with both your credit card companies and your car insurance carrier to determine if you need the extra (and usually very expensive) insurance offered by the car rental companies. This is a lucrative trade for them and the clerks can be quite pushy about signing you up for extra and unnecessary expensive insurance.

➢ For those who do not want to appear to be driving alone, a company called The Safety Zone offers a bizarre but potentially useful product called the Safe-T-Man. This is the catalogue description: "Designed as a visual deterrent,

———— ✶ ✶ ————

Once on the Autoroute in France, driving from Brussels to Paris, I filled the gas tank with the cheapest fuel at the station. I should have read the sign on the tank and checked my phrase book because I filled the car with diesel. After a few miles, the car started sputtering and barely made it to the next gas station where they drained the diesel and filled it with regular.

◆

Anonymous

Safe-T-Man is a life-size, simulated male that appears to be 180 pounds and 6 feet tall to give others the impression that you're protected by a male guardian while driving in your car." Safe-T-Man has a moveable plastic head, wears a black baseball cap and sunglasses, and can be deflated for easy portability. You can dress him to suit the weather and occasion. Safe-T-Man has developed a cult following—figuring in art and literature. He can be difficult to find. Look for him with an internet search.

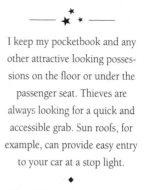

I keep my pocketbook and any other attractive looking possessions on the floor or under the passenger seat. Thieves are always looking for a quick and accessible grab. Sun roofs, for example, can provide easy entry to your car at a stop light.

◆

Brenda Davis, family manager

➤ If someone is hanging around your parked car when you return to it, walk past it as you assess the situation. If you have any doubts, summon help. Do not give the benefit of the doubt to a potential robber or assailant.

➤ Park close to well-lit exits in closed and underground garages.

➤ Avoid road rage by steering clear of the behaviorally

If I'm driving, I take my dog with me and if the motel allows dogs, then I stay there and if not, I just keep driving. I try to avoid people when I travel. I go cross-country a lot. I have my routes planned so all my friends know what route I'm taking and who to call if I break down.

◆

Kat Gonzales,
911 dispatcher

impaired on the highways. Keep your profile low on the road with simple courtesies: save your horn for emergencies, use the passing lane only for passing not for cruising, don't sprawl across two parking places, use your high beams only when they won't distract other drivers, and don't tailgate other cars.

I drive to Kansas all the time by myself. I always make sure I have enough gas to get me through to the next place that's well-lit. I never stop at the roadside rests because there are so many transient people there. If I have to stop and sleep, I stop at truck stops. And I always make sure my doors are locked.

◆

Connie Bennett, businesswoman

Chapter Five

DEALING WITH OFFICIALS

They think it rude to laugh, but they never hesitate to yawn.

—*Lady Anne Wilson,* Letters from India *(1911)*

*S*oon after the attacks on the Pentagon and the World Trade Towers, I was returning to California from Vermont, forced to transfer at the Cincinnati Airport. The Department of Homeland Security had just raised its terrorist warning level to Orange Alert. Security at the airport felt as tight as a prison. Alarm wands were cranked up to their highest sensitivity and kept screeching. Shoes off. People scrambling to find their possessions in plastic bins.

We were three hours early for the plane and hungry. We found a place that specialized in spaghetti with chili. For Lent or vegetarians there was a meatless version. Strange, it was served with oyster crackers. Even stranger, it was good. I went back for a lemonade when something louder than usual came over the loudspeaker.

"I think we'd better go hear this," I said.

The announcement came through even louder and confusing.

"We think there has been a break in security in Terminal A." Our terminal.

"Let's get out of here and go over to Terminal C. What do you think?" I suggested.

No time to think, for still louder was another announcement: "There was a breach in security and everyone must evacuate." That was it. No further instructions.

People began to mass and move. Hundreds. At first I wished to feel as blasé as those who ignored the order and were still sitting with their drinks and steaks in TGIFridays. Perhaps they were ordering triple margaritas in case this was it. No one knew. A bomb found? A suicide mission about to blow the place up?

Now we were shoulder to shoulder, heading for the exit. Thousands behind us and who knows how many in front, all following the others not knowing where we were going.

"I'm never coming to Cincinnati again, I mean I could have gone through Denver," one burly guy said to no one in particular. The fear was almost silent. Time passed as if you were waiting for the results of a biopsy.

"Where are we going?" one woman asked.

No one knew, all of us forced lemmings. Would the place soon blow up? We were underground now, marching under the runways towards the main terminal, or so it seemed. Still nothing more from the loudspeakers as we came to an unexplained stop. Impossible to move. No emergency exits to be seen. There had to be thousands of us behind and in front.

"This is unnerving, isn't it?" one woman asked me.

"Yes," I agreed.

One woman simply listened to her radio on headphones, some sports game. Kentucky was winning, and she smiled and cheered them on.

At the bottom of two escalators I chose the one that functioned. The other didn't move. At the top the march stopped again. People piled up behind us trying to push forward. As we spilled off the moving stairs people were, as the old Kingston Trio song put it, "Back to back, belly to belly."

At last we moved again, then finally out. Air, breath. I asked a woman from Delta Air Lines, "What next?"

"Everyone has to go through security again," she said. Across the street thousands were doing just that.

"How long?" I asked her.

"We don't know. Four hours, maybe."

No way to make the plane connection to home and no way was I going though that again this day. A Holiday Inn van showed up. An easy way out and we got in. I didn't care where. My instinct was not to be at the airport—I didn't care where the hotel was—I just wanted to get out of there.

In the van, stories started about who caused what everyone was calling "The Breach." One man insisted it was all because of a deaf boy with a teddy bear.

A charge card got a room right away. Soon the Holiday Inn bar was packed with people eating and drinking. Stories kept flying around the room, but no one really knew what happened.

When something seems amiss and out of my control, my survival rule is to do all I can to distance myself from the locale. I stay calm, remove myself, and worry about rebuilding my itinerary later.

Officials are often unhelpful, and usually the best thing you can do is try to make your point without creating a confrontation, as I did once when I was living in Germany.

The light changed on the Berlin street and as the traffic started to move I felt my VW camper bumped and scraped by the flat bed trailer truck in the lane next to me. After it hit me, it kept going, around the Golden Angel circle in the Tiergarten. I honked my horn, chasing after the truck.

I was thinking hard about what I'd say when I did catch

up with it. I'd just moved to Germany and at this point spoke very little German. The truck kept moving and I leaned on the horn, chasing the truck. The driver was obviously trying to ignore me and just drive away. I kept after him and finally he stopped.

I got out of my bus and with my limited vocabulary said something along the lines of, "You beat my auto." But he knew what happened. The trailer created a huge scratch and dent in my VW. What he said back to me I couldn't understand.

"We'll wait for the police," I said. I waited and waited. I was not about to leave the scene to call them because I assumed he'd just drive away again. Finally a police car showed up, but it wasn't a traffic cop.

"Bitte, konnen Sie ein umfall Polizei anrufen?" I asked, pleased with myself that I was able to request the accident investigation cops. The truck driver and I stood, he next to his rig, I beside my VW, in a misting rain. The traffic police arrived within minutes and invited us into their wagon, to sit around a table and fill out the accident report. The truck driver avoided my eyes.

Herr truck driver spoke first, in German. I took deep breaths and picked up a few words. "The woman was doing something wrong. And then she...." I couldn't understand what he said next. Again he said, "And then she..." And again I couldn't understand what he was charging me with doing. He went on and on as the police studied his piles of official paperwork.

Finally I interrupted. *"Bitte,* please. May I say something?"

The truck driver was dismissed. He smiled at the police and thanked them. The procedure seemed so unfair to me, but I insisted on trying to tell my side of the story. Using my driver's license, a pack of cigarettes, and my passport for models, I demonstrated the accident on their table with a few words of

German and a crash noise. They looked at my documents and told me I could go home.

"But what happens now? Do we go to court, to a judge?" I asked.

At last, the younger cop spoke to me in English, "Don't worry, he was wrong. His company must pay. But you shouldn't have passed him."

There was no point in pushing the issue even though I hadn't passed him. I was jubilant.

As we American women travel, we must always remember that even in societies such as Germany that seem on the surface so much like our own, customs and laws can be radically different. It is usually worth the time and effort to at least obtain a cursory understanding of the laws in the countries in which you intend to travel. The American guarantee of innocence unless proven guilty is absent in most of the rest of the world, including Germany.

Many of the destinations for tourist and business travelers are directly influenced by the Napoleonic Code, the laws drafted for France by Napoleon in 1804. These statutes spread to conquered territories and were instrumental in the development of laws in much of the rest of the world. The direct result is that Americans detained in most foreign police jurisdictions are presumed guilty unless and until innocence is proven.

Avoiding confrontations with authority figures is an important goal.

Tips

> If you have an accident, prepare yourself to encounter male police. Try to stay as calm as you can. Stand your ground if

you know you're right. Be patient and expect to be on the receiving end of male chauvinism. If you are politely persistent, and allow unimportant (under the circumstances) references to your sex to pass without much challenge, you may well be able to transcend such age-old obstacles.

➢ Expect, in some developing countries, that some rogue policemen may offer to drop serious charges against you for sexual favors. Take your chances with their criminal justice system—refuse politely but firmly—and face the charges.

Take a notebook and use it not only to write in, but also to look as if you have something to do.

♦

Carol Adair,
college professor

➢ Cash bribes are part of routine business with authorities in some countries. Knowing when and how to offer to settle differences with police requires querying local residents and relying on your own intuition. Using phrases such as, "Is there a way for me to pay this fine now so that neither

In Italy, I've been told that if you're stopped by a policeman and you smell a rat, ask to see his ID. Thieves have been known to show a fake plastic police badge.

♦

Stefania Payne, marathoner

of us are delayed by a trip to the police station…" or "How much is the fine and can I pay it now…" allow you to offer cash directly to a policeman without calling it a bribe. When you are dealing with more than one cop, such an opening is riskier because one may fear the other will report him for taking the cash.

➤ Try to manipulate where you pull over if a police car signals you to stop. Seek a locale with plenty of light and action such as a busy street corner or a gas station.

➤ If you wish to carry a firearm, it is wise to make sure you are familiar with applicable gun laws. You can reduce the possibility of trouble with the authorities by keeping any weapon in a holster. In many jurisdictions a holstered weapon is not considered concealed and can be stashed legally under an automobile seat. The offices of state attorneys general and foreign consulates can provide you with details of their gun control laws.

> Customs agents in China made me take all the batteries out of my things and put them through security for me. I was supposed to be able to pick them up on the other side, but they were all mixed up and I ended up with six. I kept saying, I only need two, but they didn't understand. I also had trouble there because I had film wrapped in lead to protect it from the x-rays. Even after they understood what it was, they insisted on going through absolutely everything.
>
> ◆
>
> *Jan Fleming,*
> *AIDS educator*

➤ Similarly, if you plan on carrying Mace or any kind of pepper spray or any other protective device, know not only how to use it, but know the law—foreign or domestic—that applies to it. Mace and pepper spray are illegal in many countries. If you do take them, pack them in your checked bags.

➤ Before you go through the metal detectors at airports and wherever else you may encounter them, remove any bulky metal jewelry and other metal that may make the alarm go off. Passing quickly through the metal detector not only expedites your progress, it also keeps you from being forced into a secondary search with an official who may—for some reason—get more curious about you and your business in his or her country. Delays also allow thieves to make off with your belongings which have emerged from the x-ray machine.

➤ If you are carrying a Swiss Army knife or other tool, don't keep them in your purse during air travel. They show up in a security check of your carry-on baggage and will get confiscated unless you check them. Do not carry on things that can be interpreted as illegal or threatening.

➤ Do not blithely agree to transport or deliver anything for anyone you've met on the road.

───── ⋆★⋆ ─────

When you're traveling by rail in France, make sure to punch your ticket at one of the orange pylons by the door to the tracks. If you forget to, and you run into a conductor having a bad day, play the dumb foreigner.

◆

*Margaret Bradford,
photographer*

───── ⋆★⋆ ─────

The biggest problem with customs was coming back from Thailand and going into the Seoul airport. I got pulled out of the line and completely searched for drugs. They said that the Bangkok police had tipped them off that a woman with blond hair was carrying drugs. I was really nervous, but I had to give them all my bags and let them search me.

◆

Kirsten Wivel, student

➤ Many foreign transit systems work on what purports to be an honor system. You buy a ticket, or a pass valid for several trips or good for a period of time, and are not required to show it to anyone in order to board the bus or train.

However, periodically inspectors check for valid tickets. If you are unaware of the system or how it works and are caught without a ticket or with an expired ticket, apologize and make it clear that you are a confused foreigner. Often the guards will let you off with a warning, especially if you can convince them that you will buy a new ticket immediately. If you fail, you will be faced with a sizable fine.

➤ Take a moment to assess any order from an authority figure. Remember that some will be using their badge of office to try to take advantage of you and will consider you especially vulnerable because you are a foreigner and a woman. Try to be as matter of fact as possible and give yourself an air of importance that puts you on an equal footing.

➤ If you are arrested, demand an opportunity to be put in direct contact with American consular officials. Don't be surprised if your demand is delayed or if the Americans do not respond immediately. Request to be housed alone or with other women while in custody. Do not allow police badges to be overly intimidating. If you do not trust the policeman questioning you, ask to see his superior. Don't beg or plead. Act businesslike. Your second priority after informing the American government of your predicament is to alert a friend in the U.S., someone you know who will work tirelessly and efficiently to get you home.

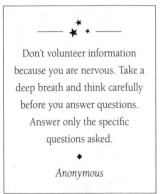

Don't volunteer information because you are nervous. Take a deep breath and think carefully before you answer questions. Answer only the specific questions asked.

◆

Anonymous

➤ If you are jailed abroad, one valuable tactic can be to publicize your plight widely in the

U.S. media. The best technique to accomplish such publicity is to rely on a trusted friend back home. If you worry you may be arrested overseas, it's best to set up arrangements for help from Stateside contacts before you leave.

➤ Never threaten foreign authorities unless you are sure of your power and are ready to risk losing the battle.

➤ If you have a dispute with a hotel or a shopkeeper that is impossible to resolve and you feel you are being intimidated, consider telling them you will call the police. Most merchants who are in the wrong, or are deliberately trying to cheat you, will not want local authorities involved and will back off from the conflict if you are about to introduce the police.

> Coming out of Russia when it was still Communist, officials looked through everything. They wanted to know why I had a book called *Hospital*—it was about Bellevue Hospital in New York. What can you do but stand there and answer the questions as briefly as possible?
>
> ◆
>
> *Annette Leyden, retired medical librarian*

➤ Your appearance can instigate unnecessary interaction with authorities. Dress and act conservatively. In some countries it is illegal, or at least frowned upon, to wear army surplus clothing if you are a foreign civilian.

➤ Guidebooks offer valuable information, but do not consider them guaranteed authority. The best of them will candidly admit that they go out of date quickly. Make sure you become your own authority by double checking crucial information such as changing laws, new government policies, and restricted locales. All U.S. Passport Agency offices provide updated travel advisories, as do U.S.

embassies and consulates. The Bureau of Consular Affairs also offers advisories over an automated fax system that is available 24 hours a day at (888) 407-4747, and from overseas (317) 472-2328, via the mail from the Office of Overseas Citizen Services, Room 4800, Department of State, Washington, D.C. 20520, or at their website at http://travel.state.gov

➤ When conditions are particularly dangerous, as long as you don't mind the government knowing where you are tramping, it is worthwhile keeping the closest American consul informed about your wanderings. If you disappear, they may help organize a search. U.S. consular help varies widely country to country, official to official, ranging from lifesaving to anemic and useless.

➤ Try to obtain general letters of introduction from officials or business figures of the countries you are visiting. Sometimes these can be used to help you out of tight spots.

★ ★ ★

The worst experience I had was traveling from Turkey back to America a few years ago. We always bring food back from Turkey because most of the stuff you can't get in America. The food we were bringing back was legal. We marked it on the customs forms. But just because we marked that we had any type of food with us, the officials went through our clothes, even our underwear, everything. They even opened all the food just to make sure that nothing illegal was being snuck in. When we were putting my clothes and the food back in the suitcase they didn't bother to provide any other containers (because they opened the cans and they obviously had juices in them) so they spilled all over. My clothes and everything were almost ruined. We complained but nothing happened.

◆

Defne Ezgi, student

Chapter Six

LODGING

The houses are in the water, and look dirty and uncomfortable
on the outside; the innumerable quantity of gondolas, too, that
look like swimming coffins, added to the dismal scene. Venice
on my arrival struck me with horror rather than pleasure.

—*Lady Elizabeth Craven,* A Journey through
the Crimea to Constantinople *(1789)*

⸻

*G*uidebooks can be quite wrong. Always second guess your
guidebook with your feelings and on-the-spot information you get from other travelers or trustworthy locals.

In a pouring rainstorm in Wellington, New Zealand—
guidebook and map in hand—I found my way up and down
the hilly San Francisco-like streets to an old Victorian guest-
house. The guidebook suggested a congenial atmosphere,
rooms with private baths, and a bargain price. From the outside, the place looked rundown, so even though I had made a
reservation, I decided to inspect the room.

I rang the bell and told the fellow my name. He led me
through a dingy hall and down into a half basement where he
opened a door.

"Here's the room," he smiled, "and the ladies is over there."
He pointed to the communal toilet facilities. The room smelled
terrible, looked worse: dirty, with a late-Goodwill decor.

"The guidebook says the rooms come with bathrooms."

He frowned and said, "We're a budget hotel. No private
baths."

I asked the price.

"Eighty-nine dollars, plus GST." GST is the ubiquitous New Zealand Goods and Services Tax, a substantial hit added to everything that would bring this dingy room in at over a hundred dollars. That would be ten more than quoted over the phone and more than the guidebook predicted. Besides, the place was unacceptable.

"Thanks," I said, "I'll talk to my partner about it."

He scowled at me. "There are other places down the street. Look for a place called the Thomas Cook. That should suit you," he said sarcastically.

As we looked for the Thomas Cook, we saw signs on some elegantly refurbished Victorians offering daily, weekly, and monthly accommodations. We hailed a woman walking out of one of them.

"Hello. Do you work here? We need a place for the night."

She stood in the rain in her windbreaker and red sneakers, telling us that she did indeed work for the outfit and was walking down to the reservations office. She started to explain complicated directions to the office.

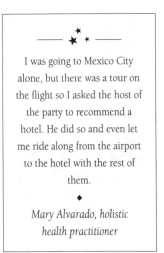

I was going to Mexico City alone, but there was a tour on the flight so I asked the host of the party to recommend a hotel. He did so and even let me ride along from the airport to the hotel with the rest of them.

♦

Mary Alvarado, holistic health practitioner

"Do you want a ride? Get in out of the rain," I suggested.

We drove up to the main hotel and office, and the place looked well over our budget.

"These nice people," she said to the desk clerk, "gave me a ride out of the rain and need a room for the night. Maybe there is one right here so no one needs to go back out into the rain."

The clerk's fingers clicked on the keys of the computer terminal while I suggested the hotel might be too pricey for us. The clicking continued and we stood there together without any more words, we three women.

"How about an apartment for a hundred dollars including taxes?"

"Great," I said, "I'll take it. Thanks to both of you."

Two bedrooms, two bathrooms. Elegant. A washer and a dryer for our road-dirty clothes.

As I sat in the living room, I looked through the guidebook. I discovered the Thomas Cook is one of the most expensive hotels in Wellington. I felt like calling the guy back at the dump up the street and describing my bargain suite at half the price of the Thomas Cook. Instead, I walked over to my kitchen and took a cold beer out of the refrigerator.

If it seems too good to be true, it probably is—especially on the road. While staying at a Mexican tourist hotel in Xalapa, Veracruz, I saw a classic colonial-style building with a banner announcing the remodeled hotel was now open. The price was one-third of the resort hotel. It was quiet, and featured a beautiful courtyard landscaped with tropical plants and tiled walkways. It seemed perfect. A woman showed me to a small but nice room, and breakfast was included at any time I wished to eat. I checked out of the tourist hotel and took my luggage over to my new dream place. The señora was not around, but at last I found a caretaker who took me to my new room.

The hotel was so new, no one else was staying there. As I unpacked I learned the house rules. The hotel was open twenty-four hours a day, but the gates from the street into the courtyard were never locked. My room looked out onto that courtyard. The caretaker handed me my keys. I locked my door and opened the charming wooden shutters covering the wide double windows. There was no glass, just the shutters. The room needed an airing. I quickly realized it reeked of fresh paint.

It was easy to open those charming shutters. They were not equipped with locks. That meant that someone could walk in off the street and simply push open the shutters to gain access to me and my belongings. I dug into my suitcase and pulled out two rubber doorstops, devices I carry to jam under doors if I worry the locks are inadequate. There was no sill on the windows to lodge the doorstops against; it was not possible to use them to secure the shutters.

The longer I stayed in the room, the stronger the smell became from the paint. My head began to ache. The señora was still absent and now the caretaker was nowhere to be seen either. Lugging my suitcase, back I went to the noisy and expensive but now comforting tourist hotel. It felt like a homecoming to me: there was my restaurant, my saloon with live Cuban music, and a door with a secure lock. Well worth the price. The next day without question my money was refunded by the owner of the renovated pension who well knew that his was not yet a finished place.

"Perhaps next time," I told him, and I told myself, "Look before you leap. Carefully, and smell, too."

Tips

➤ Register in hotels with your last name and first initial. Do not advertise your gender with your first name or a Miss, Mrs., or Ms. title.

➤ Using the stairs can isolate you in a lonely stairwell. Take the elevator, but make sure you're happy to go up or down with whomever is already in the elevator.

➤ Don't leave your room key (with the identifying hotel name and room number) on a bar while you're drinking or on your restaurant table while you're eating. You don't need to help a con man find you later, or come on to you with a line that includes information (your hotel name and room number) that confuses you because you don't understand how he got that private information.

> Whenever I go to a city where I've never been before and haven't had much contact, I find out from a guidebook or travel agent what the best hotel is and I stay there. It's mostly for safety reasons—that way I know I can avoid bad neighborhoods.
>
> ◆
>
> *Michelle Oltman, wine importer/exporter*

➤ If you fear someone is following you, don't go to your room. Go to the front desk and ask for an escort to your room. Usually that will intimidate the follower. If you're still concerned, tell the hotel employee and return with him or her to the front desk before you arrive at your room, so the predator won't learn your room number.

➤ If you're using a laptop computer to keep in touch with the homefront, be aware that some hotel telephone systems won't respond to your modem because of complications caused by the switchboard system or by digital phone equipment. Most hotels these days use a direct line to connect with credit card companies to obtain authorization for charges. If your room phone balks at making an e-mail connection, ask the desk clerk to let you plug directly into the credit card line and simply dial the log-on number directly.

➤ Some hotels offer computer users a special jack, but if you unplug the telephone to hook up your computer to check your e-mail, remember that means the telephone can't ring. You might think if you're traveling alone and no one knows where you're spending the night that it doesn't matter if the phone can't ring. That's wrong. If there is a fire or other emergency in the hotel, the hotel staff may well use the phone to warn you.

➤ There are almost as many different telephone connector jack sizes as there are countries in the world. The American standard is the RJ-11, but without an adapter for the system used by the country in which you're traveling, it will be difficult to access your computer network. Either take along adapters (available from travel and electronic equipment stores) or use an acoustic coupler, a device that fits onto the phone's mouthpiece and earpiece instead of directly into the phone line. One company that stocks just about all possible adapters is Austin House, available at (800) 268-5157.

My friend Kitty and I decided to take a motel room advertised for twenty-five dollars. She was trying to open the door when a bunch of guys came out of rooms on either side of ours. They were all around Kitty— not nice—saying, "Hey, you need some help opening your door?" We finally got in the room. We could hear through the walls; they were listening to us through the vents. I was scared, but Kitty was shaking. We left. The woman gave us our money back. We made a decision then: no rooms under fifty dollars, ever.

◆

Sophie Lemaire, chef

➤ Making a personal connection with the desk clerk and concierge can be a life saver. They are instant access into the local culture and, especially if they are women, easily accessible to friendly overtures. Just let them know you are a hotel guest and that you want to know the local customs. You'll find most clerks and concierge staff eager to share suggestions, favorite sites and restaurants, and survival tips. You may even make a friend.

I usually call before I move into a hotel to find out how the neighborhood is. I often ask the manager or people who live there. If I need to park in a parking complex or lot, I try to park as close as I can to the hotel. A lot of places have security people who will escort you to the car.

♦

Erica Noffsinger, nurse

➤ Don't spread your clothes and toiletries and books so completely throughout the room that a rapid exit will be difficult. Each evening, repack most of your things even if you're planning on spending the next night in the same room. That way, if something goes wrong and you decide to leave quickly and ahead of schedule, you won't be slowed down by looking around the room for your journal or a stray shoe.

➤ Consider using the hotel safe for valuables, but better yet, leave that jewelry you need to worry about at home and travel with just what you can comfortably keep with you. If the maid steals some clothing or a few books, it won't be that big of a deal. By using the hotel safe, you're alerting the staff that you've got something of consequence to stash, and while in transit you might not want to trust the hotel staff without getting to know them.

➤ In many luxury hotels equipped with minibars, new technology that's used to keep track of the products offered for sale can result in extra charges for you even if you don't drink the wine or buy the chips. Simply moving the bottles or bags results in an automatic charge. So if you decide to look at what's offered, or remove it all to use the refrigerator for your own soda or juice, make sure when you check out that you're not charged for something you did not eat or drink. You'll know right away if you're charged, because the food and drink in the minibars is usually ludicrously expensive.

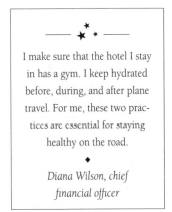

I make sure that the hotel I stay in has a gym. I keep hydrated before, during, and after plane travel. For me, these two practices are essential for staying healthy on the road.

◆

Diana Wilson, chief financial officer

➤ Fire truck ladders generally don't extend beyond a building's seventh story. Consider insisting on rooms between the second and seventh story. Ground floor rooms are more vulnerable to casual break-ins than rooms above street level.

➤ Leaving the TV or the radio on when you're out of your room makes it appear as if the room is occupied and may discourage thieves. The "Do Not Disturb" sign can trigger the same response.

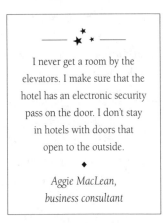

I never get a room by the elevators. I make sure that the hotel has an electronic security pass on the door. I don't stay in hotels with doors that open to the outside.

◆

Aggie MacLean, business consultant

➤ A compact and portable electric sound alarm is available that you can quickly install on your hotel door and take with you when you check out. The noise is so piercing that all but the most determined crooks will run from the pain it causes. News reporters used these effectively in Somalia. Noise alarms are also available that are triggered by compressed air; these can be used against bothersome dogs.

➤ All but the best hotels may lack adequate smoke alarms. You can buy a portable battery-powered smoke alarm at most hardware stores to take with you.

➤ If you are excessively concerned about fire and smoke, you may want to consider packing a product called the EVAC-U8 Smoke Hood. This is basically a plastic bag that fits over your head and is attached to a filter that cleans carbon monoxide and other toxic fumes out of your air supply for twenty minutes. The cost: about $70 U.S., available from travel specialty stores and catalogues. Bring it on airplane flights too; those who survive air crashes are often overcome by toxic fumes.

I was on the train to Salzburg last year and I happened to hear somebody speaking English. I asked him for his advice because he looked okay and he told me about a really great hostel. Sizing up strangers is all by the seat of my pants, but so far it's been all right.

◆

Donna Louie, scientist

I almost always have a reservation and always get a confirmation number. A flight confirmation number is essential, especially if you have to switch flights.

◆

*Tara Lynch,
public relations*

➤ If you don't trust hotel door locks, you may want to bring one of your own. The Magellan travel catalogue offers a universal supplemental lock for about $12 U.S. that can be fitted onto most doors and dresser drawers. Magellan is available at (800) 962-4943 or at their Web site: www.magellans.com. They also offer an ingenious little wedge equipped with a suction cup that can be used to block sliding glass doors.

➤ A cheap low-tech security device is a garden variety rubber doorstop you buy at a hardware store. Bring two and jam them under your door if a hotel's doors and locks seem insecure.

➤ Hotels in some countries demand that you leave your passport with the front desk overnight, either as collateral or while you are being registered with the police. Wandering a strange place without the security of your passport may be an unnerving experience and there is a trick to avoid such a predicament. The U.S. government will issue you a second passport if you can convince a consular officer or a passport office that you have a need to travel to a place where a stamp in your regular passport will cause you future problems. For example, an Israel stamp will make travel to most Arab and many Moslem countries difficult for you. Once you get that

> House exchanging is a great way to get inside a country. Not only do you usually get to live in a lovely dwelling, you may well get the use of a car along with the house, and neighbors who are excited to meet you and help you figure out what's going on. There's also a good chance they will invite you over for dinner, so you'll get inside somebody else's house, too. We have had wonderful luck doing house exchanges.
>
> ◆
>
> *Amy Valens, teacher*

second passport, leave it with hotel clerks and keep your main passport with you.

➤ Many hotels charge absurd fees in addition to local telephone company charges for calls back home, and those local telephone companies usually charge much more than American fees. If you plan to call home, get a wallet-sized card from AT&T or any of the other phone companies that lists, country by country, local numbers to call to get connected with an English-speaking operator Stateside. Then you can charge the call to your telephone company credit card or your home number.

➤ Instead of an expensive phone call, if you're not using email consider sending faxes. A detailed letter gets home for a fraction of the cost of an average telephone conversation. Include your hotel number so that your friends and family can call you back. Calls from the States are almost always dramatically cheaper than calls back to the U.S.

★

I feel very comfortable looking for housing at train stations in Europe. I don't always go to the unofficial tour guides, but I look at what the atmosphere is like and in many situations I feel comfortable going to one of the people who meets the trains. Generally I choose one who has a name tag that identifies him and can also show me a book of pictures of the places that he's representing. I know there are many people who don't feel comfortable with that, who worry that they may get taken down some dark alley. But I feel like I can identify those who are legitimate, if not officially sanctioned. I've had wonderful experiences in Rome and Amsterdam doing that.

◆

—*Amy Valens, teacher*

Chapter Seven

CHOOSING ITINERARIES
AND COMPANIONS

The difference between landscape and landscape is small,
but there is a great difference between the beholders.

—*Ralph Waldo Emerson*, Essays: Nature (1844)

———————

I rarely consider hiring a guide. But there are exceptions, and I often just find guides without asking. I've gone fishing after midnight at the edge of a campground in France with local women I met while brushing my teeth. We had few words in common, yet the feeling was so good. I don't even fish, but I held a pole, watched them and their menfolk demonstrate what I should do to catch a fish—until my feet froze. Those women were my impromptu guides.

Once in Mexico, a little boy followed the car after recognizing the California license plates. He ran alongside us, yelling.

"Missus! Let me take you—not much money—to the artists' houses. Not much money! Please!" He was barefoot, running faster.

My cynical traveling partner dismissed the boy, saying he was probably just a hustler.

But something about the look of boy intrigued me. "Let's stop the car and ask how much."

The price was so little, we followed him against my companion's wishes.

The boy took us to the home of a family that makes papiér-maché mirror frames, frames for pictures that are painted in garish colors, and other tourist trinkets. The man asked us about our work, and to show him an example of it.

"We're jewelers," I said, showing him the gold ring I was wearing with an opal set in it that I had made.

We shared stories with the craftspeople; they learned about our life and work, we experienced a behind-the-scenes look at the gross discrepancy between a Californian and Mexican artist's lifestyle. Our ad hoc guide made that possible.

In Australia, I asked for a restaurant recommendation while buying a bottle of wine at a store. The clerk pointed to a man next to me who introduced himself as a local restaurant owner. He smiled and said, "Please come to my restaurant. I used to be the chef at the best restaurant here."

I asked him what he served and he said it was just a fish and chips joint, "But I promise everything is fresh. Follow me!"

So we followed him to the little shop and he told us he'd stay open late for us, as late as nine-thirty.

Once I had a fellow traveler who stuck to me like glue. I had a one-and-a-half-hour layover, so after twenty minutes of this person not leaving me alone, I said, "Excuse me, I have to go to the restroom." When I came back, I made sure to sit between two other people.

◆

Laurie Hobbs,
computer technician

We showed up at nine and he led us to the back of the restaurant, out into the warm night, to a small table. By the time our custom-prepared food arrived—it was delicious—we were chatting with his wife, his two young daughters, and two friends who stopped by—both members of the local activist Aboriginal community. One of them fetched his *digeridoo* from his car and offered Peter and our son Michael lessons.

We were invited to their cultural center the next day for a personal guided tour, sans tourists, of the museum and bush.

In the museum I decided it best to keep my irritation to myself as I was told, and reminded by signs, that the *digeridoo* should not be played—or even touched—by women. It is their culture.

These, of course, were lucky breaks with happy endings. Often it is valuable to make use of established formal tour services.

Current information is another useful guide. Keep in touch with the local news, not only to know what events may be occurring that you might want to attend but also to keep up to date regarding changing political situations and weather that could influence you to change your itinerary.

Choosing traveling companions depends on individual proclivities. Some of us enjoy the dynamic of hanging out with groups. For those types, organized group excursions provide an opportunity to meet other like-minded travelers. The possibilities for such encounters are enormous, from the low-budget and somewhat communal bus tours run by the Green Tortoise company, to the political trips to various hot spots like the California-Mexican border organized by activists such as San Francisco-based Global Exchange, to the various classes abroad offered by many university extension programs.

I feel comfortable traveling with women. Sometimes I travel with a group if it's only women, just until I get my bearings in a country. In India I was with a group for the first ten days and by then I was comfortable with what was going on, I could see how people operated and I knew what the problems were. Then I was ready to take off and go on my own.

◆

Barbara Grosso,
teacher

If you prefer just a single companion, it's probably a good idea to choose a friend you know well so that you'll enjoy common likes and dislikes, schedules and idiosyncrasies. Remember, the one thing you can't do without in a travel companion is a good sense of humor.

Most of the time I travel alone or with Peter. I avoid crowds. I never sign up for the group tours at museums and cathedrals. I'm not interested in double dating. I like to poke around alone and discover places on my own. So I was skeptical when I was asked to join a week-long walking vacation for a writing project. Not only was this an organized group activity of the type I avoid, it meant miles and miles of walking each day. My walking routine is limited to a mile or two along the beach near where I live.

This particular walking tour was in the highlands of New Mexico, and featured walks of up to ten miles a day at altitudes above 5,000 feet, a challenge for me. One of my girl friends hikes to the bottom of the Grand Canyon and back up alone every year; I am no such type.

But I was assuaged by the details of the trip. Organized by a company called The Wayfarers, this was no "trail mix and sleeping bag" week. Overnight accommodations were in luxury hotels featuring five-course dinners. Shady rest stops along the path included fruit juice and nuts, waterfalls and naps.

Nonetheless, I had some trepidation as we started out, especially since it was clear that most of the other travelers wore hiking boots well broken in on previous long walks. But the weather was perfect and I started marching, looking forward to the first night's gourmet dinner and rest much more than the miles of desert trail.

After a few days, despite sore feet and aching muscles, I was a convert to the Wayfarers style of dealing with the wilderness. And I found myself surprised to be enjoying the congeniality of my fellow hikers. We had the walk in common and plenty to talk about at dinner. Ahead was my biggest challenge, a steep hike up to Chimney Rock. I was always the last one to arrive at each destination, and this grueling day was no exception. As usual I took plenty of time to breathe and take photographs. One woman who endlessly bragged about how many miles she ran every day decided the route was too much for her, and she was coming down the mountain while I worked my way higher. She said she just wasn't up to it. Others quit and passed me going down, too, but I was determined. I was at the end of the line, the slowest, watching my cohorts get farther and farther ahead until they were out of sight. Those who did not give up were at the summit while I was still trudging up, slipping on the scree. I only fell once, but the path was so narrow at times, my vertigo would not allow me to look over the cliff. Soon, I thought, the ones who were already at the peak would begin to pass me on their way down.

Instead when I reached the top they were all sitting there waiting for me and cheering me up the last few steps.

"Sheila made it!" one woman yelled, and they all clapped. I was touched. My simple feat was a thrilling accomplishment for me. That night we toasted one another, and they all teased me, acting as if my stated lack of experience was some joke.

Consider joining a group, especially to take advantage of the opportunity to do something completely alien from your routine. The old safety in numbers adage is true. On my New Mexico jaunt the group leader made sure we all were in place before we left in the van each day, he kept us fed and watered, and he supplied intriguing details about the history and nature of the places where we were tramping. That hike was nothing I ever aspired to do, but it now stands as one of the most memorable and satisfying trips of my life.

Tips

➤ If you do want to pay for professional tours, pick guides carefully. Get recommendations from the hotel's concierge or front desk. Otherwise consider talking with independent taxi drivers. Start by taking a short trip. Ask lots of questions, and if you feel comfortable, make a daily deal. You'll get a car and driver, a guide, and a potential protector.

➤ When you arrive in a new city, take a quick tour to familiarize yourself with what's where and what's available and what you may wish to avoid—by bus, tram, or boat. Often the public transport system provides a very inexpensive and comprehensive route around town.

> When I was in Greece, I was with a friend and we were out with a couple of guys we'd met when we landed. They had a pickup truck and my friend was riding in the back; at one point I turned around and they were gone. I totally panicked and I had the guy who was driving take me back to my room. I asked around about these two men because some of the other women at the hotel knew them and swore up and down that they were okay. She came back several hours later fine, but the experience really startled me and reaffirmed the need to communicate, know where you and your companion are going.
>
> ◆
>
> *Lisa Woldin,*
> *research administrator*

➤ Keep in touch with important news developments that affect changing travel risks. For example, a careful traveler planning a trip from Australia to England just before the 1991 Gulf War would have kept track of the increasing tension on the Iraq-Kuwait border and checked with the airline to make sure a Sydney to London flight was not refueling in Kuwait City. Sometimes travelers don't think to check where their flight across the world is scheduled to stop along the way; a troublesome stopover in some countries could be particularly problematic for women.

➤ The *International Herald Tribune* and *USA Today* are not available everywhere. Pack a small, high-quality shortwave radio so that you can keep in touch with the news from the BBC World Service (much more comprehensive than the Voice of America).

> —— ✶ ✶ ——
>
> I'm extra careful if I happen to be in any European town or city where there's a large sports event going on. What they call "soccer hooligans," often English guys, can be totally dangerous when they're on a drunken rampage.
>
> ◆
>
> *Stefania Payne, marathoner*

➤ Even if you don't want to lug a laptop computer around the world with you (or can't afford the investment in one), you can stay in touch with the news back home via e-mail and the Internet. Most cities of any consequential size these days offer cyber-cafés, or other public places such as airports, with computer terminals where you can log onto the Internet for a small fee, send and receive messages, and check for the latest news from home.

➢ As soon as you choose a spot for a stay even as short as an overnight, make yourself known to shopkeepers and restaurant operators in the immediate vicinity of your accommodations. They'll help you pick the best places to eat and sights to see, but they may also quickly come to consider you one of their own and warn you of trouble or call for help if you appear to be in danger.

➢ If you stay abroad for a while and get a job or enroll in school, consider varying your route to work or class. The sight of a foreign-looking woman, traveling regularly along the same streets, can stir the interest of predators. You will also find new neighborhoods to explore.

➢ If you travel by intercity bus and must stash your luggage in the underneath storage compartment, choose the compartment on the curb side of the bus and then make sure you sit on that side of the bus. When the bus makes stops, you can watch from the window to make sure your bags are not intentionally, or mistakenly, unloaded in the middle of nowhere, never to be seen by you again.

Two of my trips, one to Europe and one to South America, were with the same person. We sort of complemented each other. She was good with some things and I was good at others. It wasn't anything we agreed on, it just happened.

◆

Barbara Grosso, teacher

➢ If you are visiting a place where political demonstrations, labor strikes, and other mass gatherings are occurring, check with locals and the media so you can avoid them if you wish. You may wish to watch (or even join) these events, but just as is the case at home, they can be dangerous. Mob hysteria or police actions can make a benign crowd deadly in a hurry.

➤ Festivals can be not only fun, but also a wonderful window into another culture. Some events in some places do not offer a welcoming atmosphere for women. When in doubt, it's a good idea to check with local women about the customs at play.

➤ Gypsy taxis cruising for fares can pose a serious threat to women travelers, especially in poor cultures where robbing one traveler can be more lucrative than driving a cab for a year. Mexico City is particularly notorious for crimes against cab passengers. Use taxi stands at airports, major hotels, and bus stations for the safest rides.

➤ When traveling with children or teens, make clear plans for what to do in case you are separated, where to meet, whom children should be told to approach. If the children are small, dress them in bright clothes that will be easy to spot. Consider giving them a security whistle to wear around their neck, as long as they are mature enough not to blow it unless it is necessary. Children should be able to remember the name of the hotel they are staying in; if they are not, give them a business card from the hotel to carry in their pocket.

➤ When you ask questions across cultural and linguistic barriers, make sure you are simple and clear when you speak and avoid questions that require only a yes or no response. Phrase your query with constructions such as: How do I get to…? and Where is this train going…?

When I was younger, it was too hard to be two middle-aged women traveling alone. They put us at the worst tables in restaurants, sometimes there were plenty of parking places at hotels and motels, but we were told there were no rooms. So I began to join groups to China, India, Australia, all over the world, and things were taken care of for us ahead of time. Of course there were people embarrassing to be with who were rude or loud, but accommodations almost made up for that. For ten years I traveled with a woman with whom I had nothing in common. Sometimes I'd come home and say "never again," we were so different, but I realized that's what got us through difficult situations. What upset her didn't bother me at all, but when I was bothered, she wasn't upset. It worked out beautifully.

◆

Christine Shordike, retired

Chapter Eight

HEALTH

Scorpions haunt all the houses. Their bite is poisonous.
The effects are more or less violent in different constitutions.
Some persons will remain for eight days in convulsions,
foaming at the mouth, and the stomach swelled; others,
by immediate remedies, do not suffer much.

—*Madame Calderón de la Barca,* Life in Mexico *(1843)*

---

*A*s my mother-in-law never fails to remind me, "If
you've got your health, you've got everything." Health
concerns are crucial during the preparations for your
trip, even if you rarely fall ill.

Health insurance for the road is worth the investment. Just
ask Michelle Annand. I encountered her sad story in the *Otago
Daily Times* while traveling through New Zealand on my way to
Milford Sound. I read it with some peace of mind as I had
checked with my insurance carrier before I left the States and I
knew I was covered in New Zealand (or anywhere in the
world). I just needed to pay up front for any covered medical
attention and then get reimbursed once I returned home.

But Ms. Annand set off for six months in India without
insurance. All she wanted was inspiration for her work as a
painter and a chance to study classical Indian dance. For a
month all went well. Then she broke her leg.

"It happened by sleeping in a yogic position and getting
quickly out of bed," she told the *Times*. She took a step "with a
leg that lost circulation and it twisted under me," and then was

forced to endure a two-and-a-half hour taxi ride to the hospital. "I held my leg together with pillows while the taxi bumped around on monsoon-damaged roads."

For six days she languished in the hospital, her leg in a cast but not set properly and not healing. The basic necessities were a battle with an unsympathetic staff: water, bedding, toilet paper. Finally she managed to get a phone call through to her parents who arranged for a trip home and traditional Western medical care.

Michelle Annand's advice to anyone who listens is simple and direct: "Don't go to a Third World country without insurance. Breaking a leg may not be a disaster in many places, but in India it definitely is."

At home it is easy to avoid food-borne diseases. I cook vegetarian cuisine. But there were those times over the years traveling when there was no way to resist a filet mignon with some Stilton cheese sauce. That all ended for me while I was living in Europe and Mad Cow Disease became a reality in England. Shortly after one great meal with some luscious beef, the continuing headlines in the papers cured me. No longer do I eat red meat anywhere after reading exactly what this disease—spongiform encephalopathy—does to the brain. It is a horrendous death.

The U.S. Centers for Disease Control (CDC), in its guidelines for people traveling to Europe, advises avoiding beef and all beef products altogether. If you simply cannot do without a hunk of meat, choose solid cuts of muscle, says the CDC, and shun those sausages or hamburgers. The good news is that, at least according to the CDC, drinking milk and eating other dairy products does not put one at risk for Mad Cow Disease.

But mad cows aren't the only new problems to fear if you

worry about your health far from home. Severe acute respiratory syndrome (SARS) spread panic in Asia in 2003, and it is still something to watch for as you plan a trip. SARS is a respiratory virus that can be fatal. It is transmitted by close contact—that means crowded cities. The best way to avoid places plagued with SARS is to check with the World Health Organization (WHO) or the CDC. Both maintain web sites that will alert you to where SARS, or any disease, is currently a problem. Asian bird flu, or avian influenza, spread havoc when it started killing people in Asia in 2004. It spreads to humans from live poultry and their droppings, so if your itinerary includes farms or live animal markets, a check with the WHO or CDC is in order if you wish to stay away from potential problem spots. Dengue fever is another nasty disease to be aware of. It's a tropical disease, spread by mosquitoes, for which no vaccine is available. Dengue causes extreme fever, headaches, nausea, and vomiting. It can kill.

I make sure my vaccinations are current for everything and anything that might come calling to infect me where I travel. Hand washing is a must. I carry waterless hand sanitizer with me in little plastic bottles, and ever since I ran out of the gel in Mexico, I carry enough for the entire trip. I tried four pharmacies in Mexico to replenish my stock and the pharmacists just shook their heads saying they had never heard of such a product. An easy substitute that is available the world over is alcohol. It may dry out your skin, but it may save your health.

Of course sometimes there is simply nothing to do but take a chance, especially on the road far from home. In most Second and Third World countries the blood supply is not considered safe. Once I was asked to teach for a week in Brazil not long after a serious illness that required transfusions. It wasn't possible to just bring along a few pints of blood for insurance.

Instead I bought travel insurance that included medical evacuation in cases of extreme emergencies. Fortunately I didn't need to take advantage of the coverage, and just because you buy it doesn't mean it will accomplish what you expect. Under the terms of many insurance policies, air evacuation requires pre-authorization from the insurance company. You could be bleeding to death while you wait for them to answer your telephone call. Check the policy carefully and ask a lot of questions. You may also want to check to see if you already carry such insurance and do not know about it. Some of the premium credit cards come complete with insurance, and the American Automobile Association Plus card includes medical evacuation services.

Tips

➤ Even if you risk living without insurance in the USA, invest in insurance for the duration of your trip. You will be surprised at how relatively cheap short-term health insurance can be. You do not want to be at the mercy of questionable doctors speaking in languages you do not understand in hospitals with substandard sanitation.

➤ Look for an insurance policy that will pay to transport you to Western-class health facilities.

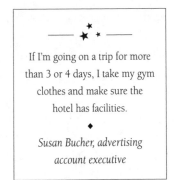

If I'm going on a trip for more than 3 or 4 days, I take my gym clothes and make sure the hotel has facilities.

♦

Susan Bucher, advertising account executive

➤ Kidnap and ransom insurance is available if you fear you may be snatched during your trip. Because the odds of such an occurrence are remote, some brokers offer as much as a million dollars worth of insurance for a premium as low as $500. Some policies offer advice from security professionals for avoiding kidnapping, trained negotiators if a kidnapping takes place, and a vacation somewhere safe once the rescue is made.

➤ Check to make sure your prescriptions are properly filled. Peter went to the trouble of getting an Imodium script (back before the anti-diarrhea drug was available over the counter) in case he got sick on a trip to the Afghan-Pakistan border. He got sick and took the pills. He got sicker and called me at home in California. I told him to read the codes on the tablets. The pharmacist had mistakenly filled the bottle with the arthritis drug Indocin. One side effect of Indocin is diarrhea.

I ran out of my medication in Portugal. I went to a pharmacy and showed the pharmacist the bottle, asking if he could refill the prescription. He did so on the spot. What a relief. I got the pills without having to go to a doctor who may or may not have spoken English. A friend of mine told me he did the same thing in Bolivia without even having a labeled bottle to show. He just asked for the medication at a drug store.

♦

Anonymous

➤ If you are a gourmand, be cautious in southern Europe about purchasing farm or home-preserved produce, such as mushrooms preserved in olive oil. Improperly canned food can contain botulism.

➤ Especially when traveling alone, consider checking in regularly with a friend or partner back home. If you're sick and miss a call, you'll know someone will become concerned. If you miss two, your contact should try to reach you. And if you stay out of touch too long, you should have a deal with your friend to initiate a thorough search. If the cost of long distance check-in calls is an inhibiting factor, come up with a simple code: call collect using a name that your contact knows simply means you are okay.

➤ In regions where health concerns are serious, check in with the American consulate. If there is no American consulate nearby, friendly nations often share in-country information with American travelers. Try the British, Canadians, Australians, and other well-traveled English speakers first.

When I run, I usually don't go off the beaten path. If you hurt yourself, you want to be in a place where someone will find you. Otherwise you could wait for days for help.

◆

Marcia Kay,
fitness coach

➤ Call the International Association for Medical Assistance to Travelers (716-754-4883) for a list of English-speaking doctors worldwide. They can also be reached by e-mail: iamat@sentex.net or visit their website at: http://www.sentex.net/~iamat

➤ Know some of the warning signs that you may have picked up a parasite: diarrhea, constipation, unusual flatulence, joint and muscle aches, anemia, allergies, skin conditions you can't figure out, sleep disorder, teeth grinding, chronic fatigue.

➤ Your period may come unexpectedly and you ought to be equipped with enough tampons and pads to last through at least one entire period. You'll be surprised at how many foreign shops are closed on Sundays and holidays with which we're unfamiliar. Even international airports might be of no help. At one important Western airport where I landed there was an apologetic note posted explaining that the tampon and pad vending machines were permanently shut down because of vandalism.

➤ Healthy pregnant travelers should be over the worst of any morning sickness by the fourth month, and full of energy at least until the sixth. Check with your doctor or midwife before any strenuous travel, of course, and don't push yourself too hard. Allow for plenty of nap times. Consider avoiding those regions of the world where health care does not meet the standards you enjoy at home. When you establish your itinerary, you may also wish to avoid those regions that would require you to take the kind of preventive medications that you would not like your baby to be subjected to through your body.

➤ If you're pregnant, stay away from traveling to exceptionally high altitudes except in pressurized aircraft. Check with your doctor about what times during your pregnancy are least risky. It is safe to say that cruises should be avoided during the final trimester—you don't want to be stranded at sea and in labor.

> Many travelers to developing countries get diarrhea shortly after they arrive, it just goes with the territory, and you'd best be prepared for it. Bring toilet paper, handi-wipes, aloe vera gel to relieve soreness, plus whatever medicines your doctor and your witch doctor recommend.
>
> *Janis Blaise, homemaker*

➢ Even healthy and fit women find that pregnancy can change their walking and running abilities. Keep to well-lighted streets with plenty of people around if you're strolling alone.

➢ If you discover that you're pregnant while traveling in remote places away from well-trained doctors and the latest medical equipment and medicines, take your vitamins and consider coming home to take advantage of modern health care facilities.

➢ On long flights across time zones and the international dateline, keep track of your biological time if you take birth control pills.

➢ I travel with an enormous stash of vitamins and food supplements collected in a compartmentalized plastic case with labels identifying each vitamin. Although it is important to consider the potential vulnerability of traveling with pills carried outside of their original containers, I am not worried about my vitamin supply. My theory is that any suspicious customs agent will be convinced that they are vitamins both because I'm not hiding them and because of their rank smell. Of course, trips along established drug-

---
★
★ ★

Before I get into any new water, I read it. It's hard to tell what lies beneath the placid surface. Are there old pier pilings, sunken ships, rocks? Are there strong rip tides or strange currents? One of the best ways to decipher what lies below the surface is to ask the local people. It's also a great way to meet someone new and sometimes a way to begin a friendship. Swimmers, boaters, lifeguards, harbor masters, and fishermen tend to be pretty friendly people and all of them can give you an idea what the lake or river or ocean is like.

◆

Lynne Cox, endurance swimmer and writer

smuggling corridors require extra sensitivity to this issue. My suggestion is that all women take along at least high-potency vitamin C, a B complex, digestive enzymes, and melatonin. Although there are some skeptics, I am convinced melatonin helps ease jet lag.

➤ For over-the-counter remedies, I suggest all women take along at least a hefty supply of both aspirin and a non-aspirin pain relief compound (if you travel with your pre-pubescent children, they should not take aspirin because of the danger of Reye's Syndrome), antacid tablets and an anti-diarrhea medication. In addition to whatever might come to ail you on the road, by bringing these medicines, you're in a position to help others you meet along the way.

➤ Other things that are so common in your medicine cabinet that you may not think to take along: Band-aids and rubbing alcohol. If your destination is even on the fringes of the First World, bring toilet paper. It is light to pack and as you use it, it leaves room in your luggage to bring back souvenirs. If you run out, even in the heart of the Third World, you can often obtain some emergency toilet paper from five-star hotels in capital cities. These hotels are also accommodating safe havens if you need to get off the street for a breather. If you act as if you belong, you can use the toilets, the telephones, browse the much-too-expensive gift shop, or just relax in a comfortable lobby chair—all for no charge.

➤ Coffee addicts should bring along Nodoze or Vivarin to fend off caffeine withdrawal headaches when traveling in areas where coffee is either hard to find or tastes so foul that it's difficult to swallow.

➤ Wash your hands repeatedly, and always before eating. Keep a stash of anti-bacterial moist towelettes (available at most drugstores) for cleaning up when the washrooms are dirtier than your hands. Keep your hands out of your mouth and eyes.

➤ Carry an extra pair of eyeglasses and a copy of your eyeglass prescription. Take along extra wetting and disinfecting solutions for contacts.

➤ Especially in hot climates, wear skirts or loose pants and cotton underpants to reduce the likelihood of vaginal infections.

Whenever I get into the water for the first time, I always slide my feet. That way if there are any stingrays on the sandy bottom they shuffle away, and if there is any glass or other debris, I may hit it with my big toe, but I won't step down and cut myself on it.

◆

Lynne Cox, endurance swimmer and writer

➤ I carry *feuilles de savon* no matter where I go. These are paper-thin leaves of soap packaged in a folder the size of a credit card and available in boutiques that specialize in skin care products. After I wash my hands, and before rinsing them, I wash the tap itself before turning it off. If there aren't paper towels available, I just shake the water off my hands.

➤ If London is a transit stop for your onward journey, an excellent resource is the chain of British Airways Travel Clinics. There are 40 of the clinics throughout the United Kingdom, including sites at Heathrow and Gatwick airports. They are open to all travelers, not only BA customers, and offer advice on health conditions in most countries of the world. The clinics provide vaccines and no appointments are needed. Clinic locations are listed on the BA Web site at www.british-airways.com/bans/lworld/clinic.htm

---

★
— ★ ⋆ —

I was about 23 and with my family on a two-day cruise down the Nile on a luxury boat when I became very sick from the food. As I was lying in the hotel room later, a guy came in to change the towels and said something in broken English to the effect that he knew how to make me better. I thought that he had some inside knowledge about people who get sick over there. He told me to roll over and in my weakened condition, I did. I felt really vulnerable and then he started rubbing my back. At that moment my stepfather walked in, looked at the situation and told this guy that it was time to leave.

◆

Stephanie Secrest, photographer

Chapter Nine

ATTITUDE

The Poles seem a lively people. The women of the lower class wear
upon their heads a wrapper of white linen, under which their
hair is braided and hangs down in two plaits. I observed several
of them with a long piece of white linen hanging round the side of
their faces, and covering their bodies below the knees: this singular
kind of veil makes them look as if they were doing penance.

—*William Coxe,* Travels into Poland, Russia, and Sweden *(1792)*

---

*T*he attitude with which you approach a situation on the road may be misperceived by others. When Poland was behind the Iron Curtain, there were strict rules for tourists. In order to get most visas, you had to pay in advance for an unseen hotel room of the government's choice. "The best hotel in Sopot," was promised us by the government-run Orbis tourist office, and the fading turn-of-the-century Grand Hotel probably was the best. There was no choice, the other hotels were off-limits to American tourists.

Swans swim directly in back of the Grand on the Baltic Sea. In the room, a colorful china platter is cemented to the wall to replace broken bathroom tiles. Holes are drilled through the platter to accommodate the bath tub spigot and the hot and cold water controls. On the inside of the door, a list is displayed in a plastic frame. The awkward translation states the house rules. The first is that no women who are not guests in the hotel may come up to the room. Another makes it clear that additional blankets cost extra.

We wander with our son Michael around the resort town and stop in a bakery to buy some bread. Peter orders. The woman behind the counter looks at me, not him, and makes it clear in terse Polish that I ought to be performing the duties of a wife. And that includes choosing and ordering the family bread. I remember only a few words of Polish, but her meaning and body language is clear. The same act is repeated in a cheese store. I am berated by the clerk who can't understand why Peter is ordering, clearly I look Polish and he doesn't.

We eat dinner in the hotel. The dining room is high ceilinged, with dilapidated elegance, the waiter dressed in frayed and formal black and white. We decide to risk still another fish from the grossly polluted waters of the East Bloc and eat a delicious meal of trout, potatoes, and cabbage salad, all washed down with a nice bottle of wine.

Peter and Michael head up to the room for the night and I order coffee and an after-dinner drink, pulling out my notebook to write. When I next look up, the waiter is sitting alone, all the other diners are gone. We say goodnight and I leave to return to the room.

Three steps up the grand staircase that curves up behind the reception desk, I hear the desk clerk speaking loudly in Polish. I keep climbing. She is obviously angry at someone. I look back again and realize that the woman's angry words clearly are designed for me. Using

I bought cheap clothes in India. I wore what the natives wore. If they wore scarves, I wore scarves. If everyone wore long skirts, I put on long skirts. It saved me from a lot of hassle. People who would normally bother tourists wouldn't bother me because it looked like I was living there and it made me more comfortable.

♦

Barbara Grosso,
teacher

85

hand gestures, she points that I should come down the stairs. I do, curious about her problem. With another furious burst of words, she points me to the door.

"Pardon me," I say in precise English, "but I don't understand what the problem is here." I pull out my room key.

"Your passport, please," she says. All clerks in the tourist hotels speak English.

"You have it. Laufer, Sheila Swan."

She apologizes. I don't bother to tell her my mother's maiden name was Soja and her mother's Kozloski. But clearly my Polish ancestry is apparent in my looks, and because of my chic Western clothing, I stood out among my distant Polish cousins. Obviously the woman initially thought she was preventing a Polish call girl from violating hotel rules.

My somewhat disdainful attitude allowed me to take control of the moment.

Rather than becoming angry in such situations, my attitude is to be calm and firm.

Tips

➤ Walk and act with a sense of confidence and purpose. Few things attract hustlers more than an obvious tourist standing around looking at a loss for what to do next.

I like to visit places during their worst weather: Tucson in the summer, Alaska in the winter, Asia in monsoon season. Different things happen, you get people in hotels and restaurants who are grateful for your business, you meet locals who are pleased or bemused that you would visit in bad weather. But be sharp, because the thermometer of the unexpected gets high. In Calcutta for instance, be careful crossing a flooded street—you might fall in an open manhole and drown.

◆

Margaret Bradford,
photographer

➤ Don't generalize; learn the specific subtleties of the region where you're traveling. Islamic culture, for example, differs greatly from one country to another. You can't go wrong in any Moslem country by dressing modestly in loose-fitting clothing that covers your arms and legs. But even though mosques in Turkey, for example, are available for visits by non-Moslems, they are off limits in Bangladesh for those who are not members of the faith.

➤ In the stricter Moslem countries, where alcoholic drinks are available only in the first-class hotels catering to Westerners, drinking in the hotel bar and restaurant alone is considered inappropriate behavior for women by local standards.

➤ When applying for visas to strict Moslem countries, improve your chances of being approved by wearing a hair-covering scarf for your visa photographs, and bringing a male companion with you if you meet with immigration officials in person.

⋆ ⋆
★ ⋆

I live in New York, so I'm always watching my back on the street. A couple of times I think I dodged getting mugged by actually turning around when somebody was too close to me. I turned around and looked at them.

When I come in the building, I make sure there is no one behind me. Once I'm sure I was in one of those schemes where someone tries to distract you and somebody else tries to pick your pocket. I just turned around and looked these people in the face. It was in a Post Office vestibule. One person was not going out the door and I think other people behind me were going to come and take my purse or take something out of my purse. I shoved this person out of the way and went out the door.

◆

Ann Rosen, writer

➤ Keep track of yourself and your belongings, especially in tourist-filled public places where one crook working in concert with another can distract you while the other lifts your valuables. Typical distractions are spilling something on your clothes or shoes, appearing to be in distress and needing help from you, jostling you and drawing your attention with apologies.

If you put out positive energy, you're going to get back positive energy.

♦

Carole Firestone-Gillis, psychotherapist

➤ You are not welcome everywhere, and in some cases there will be no specific rules, regulations, or signs instructing you to keep out. You must see and sense the exclusion. For example, most *kafenia*, the cafés in Greece, are culturally off limits for women. A woman alone can expect to be made to feel quite uncomfortable in *kafenia* and in cafés throughout the Balkans.

➤ Dress down, but not sloppy or too revealing. Fancy clothing draws hustlers who figure the expensive attire must mean there is more of value available with a little effort.

➤ If you travel with a laptop computer, chain it to something that doesn't move if you leave it in your hotel

I think people who haven't had negative experiences tend to be more relaxed and not worry about safety. I think that because I've always lived and traveled in places that are considered safe, I haven't had to watch out for my safety. I just *assume* that I'm safe.

♦

Salli Miller, businesswoman

room. A port in most laptops will connect with a lock available at computer stores.

➤ To help deal with offensive toilet facilities, pack paper toilet seat covers with you. They're available at most Stateside drugstores. Another product to consider is called Le Funelle. It is a paper funnel that makes it relatively easy and neat for women to urinate while standing into a toilet. Made of paper, Le Funelle comes in packs of four and 20 and can be ordered from Magellan's "Essentials for the Traveler" catalog, available at (800) 962-4943.

➤ In toilet stalls, keep your purse on your lap. If you use the hook on the door, a thief can grab it from over the door and run while you're stuck in the stall.

I put light around myself. And I make sure that my AAA card is paid up to date so that I've got the long distance towing. Those are my two biggies for travel in the States.

In the Amazon once, we got up the first morning and there was the uniformed guy with the gun, and the jungle beyond, and the old rickety planes. Were we frightened? Well, there really wasn't anything to do. When you're in the United States there are so many presumptions: that you can pick up a phone and call for help if something goes wrong. But out in the middle of the Amazon River it's obvious that most of the people don't live in the cocoon of safety we live in. It was one of the most important things about the trip, to just let go of trying to be in control.

◆

Rose Anne De Cristoforo, writer

Chapter Ten

FINDING YOUR SCENE

In traveling we visit names as well as places.

—*William Hazlitt,* Notes of a Journey
through France and Italy (1826)

———

A few months after the Velvet Revolution in Czechoslovakia, we arranged over the telephone to rent an apartment in Prague. The landlady told us she'd meet us outside the building at an appointed hour. We drove up and down the street, not finding her or the place.

The weather was freezing and I walked into a bar and restaurant across the street from where I thought the apartment must be located.

The bar was full of men. Working men in their work clothes, just off the job for the day, standing around with pitchers to fill with the bar's draft beer to take home after work. They drank beer in the bar before going home with the pitcher.

I stood in line. When it was my turn, I asked the man pumping beer if he spoke English. The answer was no.

The saloon was decorated with American cowboy saddles and guns. The barman wore a leather vest and a cowboy bandanna around his neck. I asked for a glass of beer and if he spoke German. No. Then he disappeared.

From the back room a woman came out. My age, smiling.

"Can I help you?" she asked in an English accent I didn't recognize.

And help me she did!

Stania was visiting her sister for the first time since the

Prague Spring fourteen years before, when she had escaped the Soviet invasion—leaving her home and family for a new life in Canada. Her sister and brother-in-law were the proprietors of the restaurant and bar.

She called out to the men in the crowded bar with their beer pitchers, asking about the address of the apartment. The debate was loud and there was no consensus. Fed up, Stania took me into the kitchen and called the number of the landlady. She spoke fast in Czech and hung up the phone.

"She will come here," Stania told me and smiled. Pointing to the woman cooking hunks of meat in a vat of hot oil, she announced, "That's my sister Elishka."

"Hello, Elishka," I called out. "My name is Sheila." Elishka spoke no English, Stania told me.

I stayed in the kitchen, with the women, as Stania talked. The landlady showed up and Peter went with her, across the street, to secure the apartment. I learned about Stania's adventurous life as a nurse in the outback of Canada, she translated Elishka's stories about the struggle to build up the restaurant business. About how they were short-staffed because her husband was home ill, and they couldn't afford to hire more help, or trust unknown workers.

The next night we returned to eat and visit. The restaurant

was jammed. After dinner, I went back to the kitchen and announced, "I'm a good cook, I can help."

"No, this is special Czech food," Stania said, chopping onions.

"I can chop onions." We worked, talked, laughed, and managed to find the time to drink a few shots of vodka together that the customers brought to us.

Elishka admired my scarf. I took it off and gave it to her.

"Oh no," Stania said, "that's terrible. Now she has to give you something." And so: an invitation to her home the next day. The next evening I returned to the kitchen and washed dishes.

Elishka laughed at me and found enough English to call me, "You crazy American." Stania translated the rest of her sister's words. "We may not have the fanciest restaurant in Prague, but we have the only American dishwasher."

I knew I had found my scene. I'd found people with whom I could relate, and a safe and comfortable homebase in a foreign city. It not only offered

In Costa Rica, I'd meet someone at dinner and they'd give me rides or invite me to their houses. It's an amazing place. I wouldn't have gone to their houses—American paranoia. I'd take rides, though. How did I decide it was okay? Instinct, I suppose.

◆

Eileen Anderson, marketing

Sometimes language problems are really not barriers, they actually enable you to learn more about people and their ways than you could by using words. I've also discovered that whenever I am traveling alone in a foreign country, it always helps to sit near families. They are used to dealing with children who have the vocabulary of a three-year-old and usually don't mind helping a foreigner who also has the vocabulary of a three-year-old.

◆

Lynne Cox, endurance swimmer and writer

me protection, but also an entry into the non-tourist daily life of the people who lived there.

Tips

➤ Pick a café near your hotel and take your coffee or tea there every morning. Stop by again for an afternoon break each day. In a day or two, you will be recognized by the waiters and waitresses. You can begin to get to know them and learn from them about their locale. You will also feel some sense of belonging by creating a familiar hangout for yourself. If you need help after a few days, the fact that you are a familiar face to the café workers will make it more likely that they will believe your story and respond to any plea for assistance.

➤ Your regular café also gives you an opportunity to leisurely observe the local women. From watching them you can quickly learn

I usually keep a small subset of the most important things in a bag that I carry with me. I usually keep books and food and water, because what's supposed to be a four-hour bus ride could turn into an eight-hour bus ride. I keep my passport in a little bag inside my clothes and keep money between my insole and my boot. Whenever possible, I choose who to sit next to on the bus, like an older woman or a woman with a kid. When I stop to rest I keep my leg through my backpack strap

◆

*Robin Plutchok, public
information officer*

I was visiting Hong Kong. We were delayed for two hours. There was another single woman traveling and we started talking. She said she had reservations and we ended up staying together. It worked out well.

◆

Donna Louie, scientist

what passes for appropriate behavior, from clothing to public interaction with men.

➤ Try to stay in one hotel for a few days at a time. You'll begin to make connections with people so that you'll develop a comfort zone for the city where you're staying.

➤ Consider taking some classes, either private or at a public university. Language lessons are a terrific opportunity to meet other women (and men) with common interests with whom you may feel safer than with people you just meet randomly on the street. These classmates could make ideal casual dinner partners or partners for testing the local dance and club scene. You may even make a good enough friend to share expenses and room together.

➤ Take your own interests and hobbies, be it weaving, bird-watching, or whatever, and find clubs or individuals who are engaged in the same activities. Such a connection can provide an introduction to homes and experiences in a safe environment.

Since I'm often working when I travel, the work I do provides me with an introduction to local colleagues and their scenes. In Switzerland I walked by a gallery and saw something which spoke deeply to me. We went inside and very unsuccessfully tried to communicate in German with the proprietor. A lady there spoke to us in English. She took us to a show of the artist and then took us to a bookstore and helped me find a book about him. I contacted the artist and we all had dinner at her house. She turned out to be a pianist, about 80, very warm and welcoming. We've been corresponding for years now. They've become like relatives and we enjoy a close and warm relationship.

◆

Susan L. Roth, children's book illustrator

Chapter Eleven

ENCOUNTERS WITH STRANGERS

Oh the earth was made for lovers.

—*Emily Dickinson (1850)*

———

*D*ating is safe when your family has known his family as long as you can remember. Or is it? The important difference with dating while traveling lies in the mores and customs of a foreign country. Or does it?

When Peter was covering the run-up to the Gulf War, he passed through Dubai and secured a copy of the advice booklet the U.S.S. *Wisconsin* printed up in an attempt to keep its sailors out of trouble during shore leave. It's written in the quaint style of a stereotypical sailor—and from a man's point of view—but the suggestions regarding casual sexual encounters (listed under the subtitle, "The Gals") are worth repeating—both for the amusing look behind the scenes of how our Navy operates, and for the reminder it contains. The following is copied verbatim from the pamphlet, typography, punctuation, and all:

Dubai is a very international city, but there are a couple of things we need to keep in mind here. Women are not treated the same as they are in the states. Some women (but very few in Dubai) still wear veils. If a woman has a veil on, DON'T speak to her or try for a "peek" under the veil, that's VERY BAD.

Rumor has it that there are some "professional ladies" but Islamic law forbids this activity so watch out.

There are, by all accounts, a lot of very nice women in Dubai (some Arabic, British, Oriental, Pakistani, Indian, etc.) Basically, unless the woman is wearing a veil, it's okay to talk to her. So...there's no reason why you can't meet that "special lady." *If you DO meet that "special"* little lady, and you find yourselves developing mutual urges, take the necessary "latex" precautions. A moment taken to don your "STDPO" (Sexually Transmitted Disease Protective Overgarment—you get 10 seconds to don it) may keep you from having your day and life ruined.

Basically, the Navy's advice to sailors works fine for adventurous women travelers, too. Perhaps you're not on vacation to date and you're not interested in dating and you want to avoid circumstances that lead to dating. The same sorts of behavior that communicate to men at home that you're not available for dating will work for you in most cultures around the world.

This book is about safety and security. Romance is about trust and magic. The guidelines for romance are the same at home and abroad. But dating and one-night stands can well cross over into safety and security concerns. It is imperative that you make the effort to learn the basic cultural differences between home and the places you travel. Showing bare legs

In Greece, another woman traveler gave me good advice: Greek men are honorable: if you say no, they accept it. The tourists, she told me, are the ones you have to watch out for.

♦

Sigrid Akkermann,
medical student

can be like announcing you are available for casual sex in some societies, similar unintended messages can be sent by drinking in public or even meeting the eyes of a strange man with a smile.

Tips

➢ Feel secure with your intuition. If you think you can read people well, don't second-guess yourself too much.

➢ As an American woman abroad, you will almost always stand out as different—often more appealing than the locals—to the resident men. Of course, this can be a plus. But be prepared for attention based on your nationality. The cliche—blondes being attractive to men in those regions where fair hair and skin are rare—is real.

➢ Consider hiding provocative or sexy clothes under an overcoat if you want to avoid attention on your way to a party.

Yeah, I've had affairs while traveling. When you're on vacation, it's as though you're on the other side of the Earth—you hardly speak the language, he doesn't speak much English, but sometimes it just happens. Fortunately for me it's always turned out okay.

♦

Katie Brown,
travel agent

If I walk into a cafe in Italy and the guy doesn't say, "I'll make an amazing cappuccino for the girl with the blue eyes," I'd consider looking in a mirror to see if something's wrong. But I never consider their pledges of undying love.

♦

Alisa Roth, journalist

➤ If you are at a bar or drinking with anyone you do not know well keep an eye and a hand on your glass. Rophynol (also known as the "date rape drug") and other colorless, odorless, and tasteless tranquilizers can be slipped into your drink by men who prefer their sex with partners who are barely conscious. Rophynol is now being manufactured with a dye so that it is not colorless but there are many other powerful drugs that are completely invisible in a drink. Don't think it can't happen to you! Some women have not even been aware that they were raped until they saw themselves later on videos confiscated by police. Do not accept glasses of punch at parties where you don't know the host well.

➤ If you expect sex during your travels, remember that, depending on your destination, condoms may not be easily available. Some countries may offer no condoms, others may be substandard for protection against sexually transmitted diseases. Condoms should be stored out of bright light and away from heat. Check the expiration dates on the packages and look for condoms that meet international standards and so are labeled with the code ISO 4074-1:1990.

When my sister and I were traveling, she was always smiling and looking in people's eyes, so I played the sour one. This confused the men who thought that my sister was asking for men to follow us.

♦

Amber Morris, singer

➤ If you wish to avoid casual come-ons from flirtatious fellow passengers on trains and buses, you'll find women-only seats in India and some of the other former British colonies, and in many Islamic countries.

➤ A relatively safe place to meet men is in group situations. These can be an opportunity to meet like-minded companions and observe them in the company of others. Consider scientific expeditions, church services, language classes, sports events, a workout gym, or museum tours.

➤ Insist on a first date in a public place, in order get to know your companion in a safe environment. Do not go off on a lonely hike in the woods or a long drive in the countryside until you feel comfortable with him.

➤ A good device to keep a new date from feeling that he can expect something from you is to insist on paying your own tab. Keep enough money with you to pay your share, but do not carry so much cash that you make yourself attractive as a potential robbery victim.

➤ Double dating is useful for insuring that you are not alone with someone new, while retaining a romantic atmosphere.

➤ Persistent unwanted advances usually will stop if you really ignore the person after once, and only once, saying no. The important part is not to respond. Do not be reluctant to reject anyone who seems threatening or pushy. The advantage when you're traveling is that you can get out of town.

When going to a Middle Eastern or Muslim country, it's sometimes safer to wear a veil, just across your hair. Also, don't look into men's eyes. Eye contact in the Middle East means that you're trying to seduce a man. Cast down your eyes.

♦

Fariba Nawa, news reporter

Chapter Twelve

WHEN A THREAT IS REAL

This is the paradise of thieves. I think the whole population
may be divided into two classes of them; those who adopt
force, and those who effect their purpose by fraud.

—*Eliza Jay, Original Letters from India (1817)*

———————

*O*ften Americans blithely travel around the world with
two dangerous misconceptions: that the protection of
the U.S. judicial system follows them across our borders and that if they do encounter trouble with a foreign government the U.S. cavalry will come riding to the rescue.
Neither is true.

Perhaps because American society has a reputation for such
violence, Americans—and this is particularly problematic for
women—are susceptible to a false impression that foreign
lands are inherently safer than their own.

Researching a project about Americans in prison overseas
led Peter to a decaying colonial-era prison in Karachi, Pakistan
where he interviewed a hapless woman from New York who
had been arrested for heroin possession. In the filthy and noisy
group visiting cell, Peter shouted back and forth with her,
through barred windows covered with wire mesh.

"It is no place for a woman to be, I'll tell you," she said
about Karachi Central Prison, "especially for a foreigner. The
grounds are terrible," she points out the dust and mud and

garbage. "Most of the time it's covered with water, so you have to walk through puddles. The food they serve you is beans and rice every day. If you have money, you can buy your own food. If you don't have money, forget it, baby. You starve to death. Some of the food they serve you has worms in it. I mean, this is no place for an American. You get diarrhea from eating beans all the time. You get a runny stomach. You have nausea constantly. You're throwing up. You get fever. Because the rice they serve you here in prison isn't clean, you have to clean it yourself. It's half-cooked. You have to cook the rest of it yourself. It's terrible."

She complained about the inadequate medical attention and explained the special pressures she faced in a Pakistani prison as a woman, including being forced to wear traditional Islamic-style clothing. "If I go outside my gate I can't wear my jeans. They won't let me. Because all the men will start staring at me and touching and everything. If it wasn't for the fact that I have a husband, I would probably be raped by now."

She recounted a story of being molested on one of her trips between the courthouse and the prison. "I almost got raped in the Black Maria, the police van that takes you back and forth. I knocked the shit out of the guy, plain and simple. He went to grab me. He tried to rip my clothes. He tried to rape me in the Maria and I just knocked him out because I am an American. I don't take no shit, you know? I'm American. I live in New York City. So I know how to handle people like that."

The more simply I travel, the safer I feel. Unencumbered, I am able to be more receptive to what is happening around me.

◆

Amy Valens, teacher

But for all her bravado, and despite the nasty nature of her crime, hers was one rotten existence. "I try to think of nice things, but most of the time all you hear is the people who are sick here in pain. You really can't think much. Most of the time I sit and cry. I try to think of nice things. But then when you do think of nice things, you end up being miserable."

She was happy for the opportunity to offer other traveling American women advice. "If you come to Pakistan, for people who like to travel, it's nice. Don't get in the business of heroin, because you're going to get in jail. Just like me."

But don't think that just because you're not in the illegal narcotics business, you are safe from the clutches of foreign police and jails. A traffic wreck in Mexico, for example, can land the driver in jail for the duration of the accident investigation.

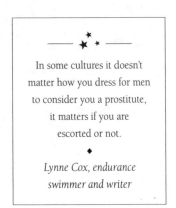

In some cultures it doesn't matter how you dress for men to consider you a prostitute, it matters if you are escorted or not.

♦

Lynne Cox, endurance swimmer and writer

My friend JoAnne's car broke down in a questionable neighborhood in Spain. She was forced to leave the car parked on the street where it stopped while she waited several days for a special-order part to arrive. Fearing loss of or damage to the car, she bought handfuls of religious cards picturing the Virgin Mary and one of the baby Jesus. These she affixed carefully all over the car to protect it, crowning the hood with the picture of Jesus. When she returned with the spare part several days later, the car was intact.

Consider the customs of the country where you're traveling to cleverly avoid theft, threats, and damage.

In some places it's next to impossible to avoid the bad guys, unless you simply stay away from those places. Obviously dark alleys, threatening-looking neighborhoods, and empty streets are all the types of spots best left alone both at home and abroad.

But you might not suspect the Tokyo subway at rush hour as a haven for sexual predators. In an article for *The New York Times*, reporter Sheryl WuDunn interviewed one Samu Yamamoto, a middle-aged man who rode the Japanese subways grabbing at women—and who shared molestation tactics with colleagues. "When men and women are packed together, squeezed onto a train," he explained, "I think everybody has some kind of desire to touch someone else's body." Women passengers told reporter WuDunn stories of having their bras unhooked and being rubbed against by men, but being so tightly packed into the cars that they couldn't defend themselves or move away from their attackers.

My friend Lee Lapin is a safety and security professional, traveling the country running seminars and workshops about all manner of tactics and techniques. Lee's intriguing book *How to Get Anything on Anybody* is encyclopedic. We got together over crabs and clams at a beachside restaurant in California to discuss attitude as an element of safety and security for women travelers.

"What about turning on the tears," I asked Lee as we contemplated the desert menu. "If a woman could summon tears at will, is that a worthwhile protective device to try to stop an attack?"

The answer came without hesitation. "It's hard to do unless you're an actress and it's probably of very limited value. Somebody who really wants something doesn't care if you're crying or not."

Screaming definitely is in a different category for Lee. "Screaming often has a shock affect on the attacker and it's probably better to scream than not, in any case I can think of. Screaming may or may not bring help, but it may buy you a second or two of time because the guy—let's assume it's a guy—doesn't expect it. That's one of the reasons martial artists use a loud cry, it kind of stuns the person for a second, gives you a split second to do something. And of course, it might bring help, if you happen to be in a place where people help screamers."

Lee studies martial arts, owns a wide variety of firearms and knows how to operate them—even shoots them on ranges for fun—and is emphatic about the importance of being familiar with weapons, if a traveler decides to take one on the road for protection. "It's wise to sit and review times when you were stressed or afraid to see what your reaction was. If you feel you want to protect yourself with something, look for mechanical things like whistles or mace,

I always wear running shoes,
I never wear something I
can't move fast in.

♦

Marilyn Byus,
planner

whatever would be allowed where you're traveling. Then get practice using it. Learn limitations. Learn both your limitations and the things that may help compensate for your limitations."

Some of Lee's specific advice includes learning that a weapon, pepper spray for example, is not a cure-all, that it does not stop some people who are extremely drunk or on some types of drugs. You need to be close enough so that the spray affects your attacker. You want to plan an escape route so the gas does not impair your ability to run away. "Spray it on a wall and stand next to the wall to get an idea of what it feels like," Lee suggested. The same sort of familiarity is crucial for any weapon you contemplate carrying, or picking up, such as a club or a stone.

We talked about appearance. Is a pretty woman more likely to attract attackers than a Plain Jane? Lee was less concerned about subjective beauty than appearance as it relates to why a predator may be interested in targeting a specific traveler.

"If you look like you might have money, if you look drunk or available for a casual pick-up, you're much more likely to get hit on." Lee's advice is specific: take off your jewelry, don't display things other people really want, don't wear pierced earrings that can get pulled out of your ear. But Lee rejects the idea that physical looks play a role in vulnerability. "I think the factor is more in your bearing, your walk, your attitude, the way you carry yourself, than what you actually look like."

Perpetually anticipating the worst would make for a depressing vacation, Lee pointed out, and used an old friend's experiences in Asia as an example of how standing out in the crowd is not necessarily to be avoided. "Her hair is bright red. She trekked through Nepal and got a kick out of everyone coming up to her and touching her hair. They'd never seen hair like hers before. She was fine with it. If you mind that kind of attention from people when you're not sure of what their motives are as they approach you, if that's going to bother you, I would take any real significant feature and downplay it. Put a hat on or whatever."

I know a woman who would just start talking gibberish and act like a crazy person and she could just ward off all kinds of people, they would just run.

Fay Faron,
private detective

What about a worst case, I asked Lee. If you are physically

attacked and you do not have a weapon, should you grab for sticks and rocks, even if you have no street fighting experience? The answer came without hesitation. "If you are at the point where you can no longer run and a physical battle is going to transpire, always use a weapon. Use any weapon at hand. A rock is fine. It extends anybody's capabilities. You don't have to be a rock-throwing artist to use a rock. Swing hard and aim for someplace where it would hurt. You can take somebody down with it. Don't worry about your attacker disarming you and using it against you. He can pick up a rock just as easily as you can, why does he need your rock? People I know who fight well, even good martial artists, adhere to the rule: if there is a weapon there, use it."

Animals offer a different challenge, warned Lee. Wild animals easily interpret an unknown human in their midst as a threat. "Never look a gorilla in the eyes," advised Lee. "Don't show your teeth to monkeys, they think it means you're going to bite them and they will bite you first. You can learn about specific wildlife for the regions you expect to visit." Lee says dogs the world over respond to the same general attitude. "Don't appear challenging, don't appear frightened and run. The best thing to do is keep going your own way and ignore them as much as possible. Don't stop and confront them. Without running, remove yourself as best you can. If it degenerates, pepper spray is pretty good on dogs. Climb a tree, pick up a rock. Dogs know what picking up a rock means. Many of them will then stop, not all of them."

Women traveling on business are probably at less risk than the backpacker, according to Lee, if only because they'll be in better hotels and riding in taxis instead of city buses. "On the other hand, you'll probably be carrying a two thousand dollar computer. The number one stolen items in the world right now are portable computers. You're advertising that you do have some money when you carry a computer. Try to put it in a bag that doesn't yell computer. Put it in a brown shopping bag instead of a nice flashy computer case with your initials on it. Be very careful about people following you to your hotel room, maybe not to get you but to burglarize the room once they understand you're carrying some valuable things with you. Computers and cameras are very valuable, and not just in Third World countries, in Los Angeles too."

Lee had another piece of advice for traveling business women that doesn't apply directly to physical safety, but certainly pertains to financial security. Watch out for a devious telephone scam based on phone companies that bill your telephone account for the time you spend calling a specific number. Here is how it works. The con artists manage to get your pager number, or your voice mail number. They page you overseas or leave you a voice mail and announce a number for you to call back. The number is outside of the United States, but the area code appears to be a U.S.-type. It is three digits and the number following it is seven digits, the same configuration as in the U.S. If you answer the page or message and call the number, the operator who answers tries to keep you on the line as long as possible, and the charges can be extraordinary, as high as fifty dollars a minute. Since the company is not in the U.S., it is not subject to U.S. regulations.

"What they do," Lee explained, "is buy a list of pager numbers, cell phone numbers, people with voice mail. They call and leave a very frantic message saying things like, 'Your husband is injured, call this number right away please!' or they'll put the call back number on your pager and leave 911 after it a few times. Then once you call you'll get put on hold and it can end up costing several hundred dollars if you don't successfully dispute the charges with the phone company that bills you."

Lee Lapin looked over the dessert menu one more time, decided against the chocolate truffles and the cheesecake, and got up from the table with a final warning. "Don't trust any deal that looks like it's too good to be true."

But don't worry too much about *foreign* surroundings. Remember these sobering domestic statistics from the U.S. Department of Justice: nearly 75 percent of sexual assault and rape victims say that their assailant was not a stranger.

Tips

➤ Guns, and even mace, are illegal in many destinations. But there are other methods for self protection. Consider learning a martial art. This will be a valuable tool while traveling, as well as at home. Remember that if you carry a weapon, it could be turned against you.

➤ Prepare yourself for the worst. Consider a rehearsal, with friends or in your mind, of an attack. Learn how you would react to a gun in your face or a knife at your throat. Survival courses that include simulated danger can be found through adult education schools in most metropolitan areas. These can include everything from judging body language to weapons training.

➤ Noise is effective. Practice screaming before you leave home. A healthy scream can scare an assailant, draw attention to your predicament, and bring help. Do not be afraid of making a scene.

➤ Loud whistles are another effective tool for scaring attackers and summoning aid. Consider wearing one as a necklace. Just be sure that you can grab it easily. A noise-maker buried at the bottom of your purse is worthless if you have to dig for it during a crisis.

➤ As the characters in *Monty Python* suggest, if you are attacked, "Run away, run away, run away!"

➤ If you are attacked and decide to fight back, do everything you can to hurt your assailant. Aim for the eyes, solar plexus, and throat. Pull hair. Bite. Scratch. Remember the extreme vulnerability of a man's testicles. Grab and squeeze as hard as you can, as a woman I met in the desert once did. The man who was after her was hospitalized, never to bother her again. If possible, tear your attacker's clothing and other possessions to mark him for later police identification. Above all make noise, lots of excruciatingly loud noise.

➤ If you appear vulnerable to predators, you are more

—— ✦ ✦ ——

I have a friend who takes a stun gun and pepper spray when she's hiking. She has another thing that beeps loudly and she keeps all these in her backpack. In a really dangerous situation she couldn't get them out fast enough to help herself. But, I think the city is more dangerous than walking in wilderness areas.

Much of it is attitude. As much as I travel alone, I've never had a problem. I don't do stupid things. When you watch those old horror movies where the woman goes into the basement alone in a strange house, well that's stupid.

◆

—*Casey Landry,*
businesswoman

likely to be victimized. Know your strengths and weaknesses. If you're out of shape, you're obviously going to be hard-pressed to outrun or fight off an attacker, so you may want to be more cautious than your marathon-running sister about bad neighborhoods and questionable circumstances.

➤ Be judicious about taking photographs. What may seem to you a simple tourist snapshot can be interpreted as a spy picture in some places. Stay safe by keeping your camera pointed away from military installations, airports, train stations, international border crossing points, and anyone in an official uniform. Even bridges and power generation plants are restricted for photographers by some oppressive governments. If you really want a picture of such things, seek specific approval from an authority you are convinced is in charge.

> ─── ✦ ✦ ✦ ───
>
> In Washington, D.C. once we had some creepy guys following us. We went from place to place and hid. After a while, they got the hint—we weren't going to be easy targets.
>
> ◆
>
> *Sonja Walker,*
> *finance manager*

> ─── ✦ ✦ ✦ ───
>
> We were walking in New York and someone said, "You shouldn't walk here," so I flagged down a policeman. He said, "Even I don't walk here," and he drove us home.
>
> ◆
>
> *Renate Moore,*
> *retired*

➤ Binoculars also can be interpreted as spy paraphernalia by paranoid regimes. Avoid pointing your bird-watching glasses at army bases and police stations.

➤ Just as at home, elevators can be a vulnerable locale for a woman alone. If the door opens on a floor before yours and someone gets in who makes you feel uncomfortable, do not hesitate to get out. Similarly, do not get into an elevator if the passengers already inside seem at first glance like the wrong crowd. There's almost always an emergency button to ring.

➤ Be wary about riding alone in train compartments, especially at night. At the same time, balance that concern by choosing your compartment companions with care. Of course that requires snap decisions based on appearances, another reminder that your instincts are often your best protection.

➤ The U.S. State Department lists countries it considers dangerous for U.S. citizens and it is well worth checking with them to hear their latest warnings. These advisories are quite specific and could either help you avoid dangers or convince you to change your itinerary because of specific threats against women. For example, prior to the tragic highway robbery and rape in Guatemala of a group of Maryland college students, the State Department warned that "shootings, rapes, and violent assaults have for the most part occurred during daylight hours and in many cases have affected entire groups of American tourists. Highway travel has generally exposed visitors to increased risk of violent incident."

Sad, but true, I feel safe the minute I get out of America. Even if my purse is threatened my person is not.

♦

Susan L. Roth, children's book illustrator

➤ Harassment is common for women travelers to Italy, especially in the south, as it is in other countries where *machismo* is a continuing cultural factor. Avoid sleeping in train stations and other public places where you could be vulnerable to assault, and do not count on the police to be free of the tendency to grope and fondle foreign women.

➤ It can be crucial to learn local customs and laws quickly. Watch your feet in Thailand where it is rude if they point at another, and be careful about touching the heads of other people—the head is respected as holy. Buddhist monks are not supposed to interact with women, so you should not touch or even be adjacent to them. Drug smuggling in Thailand, Malaysia, and some other Southeast Asian countries can result in the death penalty.

➤ Few countries are as inhospitable to single women as Saudi Arabia. If you go there it will not be as a tourist, no tourist visas are issued. It is illegal for women to drive rental cars. The sexes are segregated on city buses. Penalties for bringing pornography into the country are severe, and what might be considered by

> I was flying into San Antonio and I had a layover in Dallas. It was late at night and this man just kept following me. It didn't dawn on me at first, but I'd go into the bookstore and he'd follow me. When I got on the plane, he did too and when I got off, he followed me to baggage claim and asked me where I was staying. The airport was deserted, so I walked over to a woman sitting in a booth for shuttle service and just stood right beside her. He finally went off to bother some other lone woman.
>
> ◆
>
> *Jennifer Ricciuti, technical trainer for software design firm*

you to be a picture of a woman in a sexy outfit could well be considered to be pornography by Saudi customs officials. If you dress in what is considered immodest clothing in public places, you face abuse from the so-called religious police.

➤ If you enjoy a mane of luxurious hair—especially blond in countries where most women are dark-haired or cover their heads—it's an attention getter, and not always the type of attention you seek. One solution is to simply keep it tied back and covered.

➤ Are beautiful women more likely to attract unwanted attention than Plain Janes? Not necessarily. Their very attractiveness may help protect them because they might appear unapproachable. But this assumption is not fool-proof protection, especially in the face of groups of men who may perceive the display of feminine beauty as immodest behavior.

➤ If the people don't scare you, the animals might. Without being paralyzed with paranoia, it is worthwhile to consider the potential dangers of animals in the road. We know a woman who travels with a pocketful of dog biscuits to pacify pariah strays. It's usually a good idea to avoid direct eye contact with any animal that appears threatening. A walking stick can provide you with a weapon against attack.

➤ For a complete listing of the types of deadly animals you can encounter while traveling, consult John "Lofty" Wiseman's book, *The SAS Urban Survival Handbook*. He tells stories about critters like the candiru, a skinny little South American catfish. The candiru is attracted by urine and likes to enter humans through urogenital body openings.

The rear-pointing candiru spines cause great pain to the victim. "Wear tight protective clothing over genitalia," advises Lofty, "if tempted to bathe in suspect rivers and streams."

➤ Learn the psychology of scams and scam makers. They prey on the average person's reluctance to accuse another of wrong-doing, or even the intent to commit a crime. The same is true with purchasing scams. Whether it's trying to get you to buy mosaics in Agra, carpets in Morocco, shoes in Italy, or emeralds in Rio, there are some very clever people out there who are not actually criminals, but who are so skilled at manipulation they should be avoided.

➤ Fear can be your ally. This is the central theme of Gavin de Becker's book, *The Gift of Fear*, which was discussed in Chapter Three. If you walk into your hotel room and your things are not as you left them, then fear is an appropriate response and should motivate you to leave the room immediately and seek help. That sort of fear, based on a specific threat, is empowering, as opposed to the kind of generalized fear which is like phobias about the unknown.

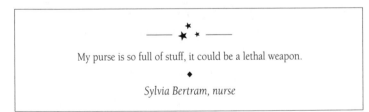

My purse is so full of stuff, it could be a lethal weapon.

Sylvia Bertram, nurse

Chapter Thirteen

IF YOU BECOME
A VICTIM

I made a short cut for it and the next news was I was in a heap,
on a lot of spikes, some fifteen feet or so below ground level,
at the bottom of a bag-shaped game pit. It is at these times you
realize the blessing of a good thick skirt. Whereas, save for a
good many bruises, here I was with the fullness of my skirt tucked
under me, sitting on nine ebony spikes some twelve inches
long, in comparative comfort, howling lustily to be hauled out.

—*Mary Kingsley,* Travels in West Africa *(1897)*

*M*ay in Spain. For a birthday present, I found a three-week live-in Spanish language school on the Costa del Sol. Each day after the six hours of studying and eating, a group of us would head down from our bucolic village to the public beach.

Hugo and Ines, who had studied at the same school the year before, warned us of the robberies they had heard about, especially near Malaga. Lock your car, they said, keep it in sight as much as you can.

One hot day we parked our VW bus between the coast road and the dunes, and piled out for a nice spot on the sand. As is usually the case, I was not much interested in swimming, going into water where tampons washed up on the shore as part of the flotsam. And fair as I am, I tried to stay pretty covered up on the beach. So I sat in white clothes on a towel. But this day became just too hot even for my light summer whites.

"I'll be back in a minute or so," I said to Ines. "Please tell

Peter and Michael." They were playing Frisbee down the beach. Ines was topless and, as always, found it funny that I kept my clothes on. "I'm going to the bus to change into my bathing suit."

I got into the bus, found something to eat, drew the curtains, ate and changed. I stayed only a few minutes and then carefully locked the sliding door before I headed back to the beach and joined the others— just out of sight over the dunes. Not more than a quarter hour later, we all were hungry and packed up our gear to head into town and buy food for dinner.

Peter got into the driver's seat and immediately noticed that the wing window on the passenger side was open. A quick look around and we saw that the car had been ransacked. His suit was stolen. Binoculars, camera, tape recorder: gone. Michael's toys were still in the bus, along with some other more valuable things. Perhaps the thieves saw us coming and ran?

A break-in is a nasty violation of your personal space.

I had one bad experience in San Jose, Costa Rica. I was in a bus terminal, I had my brother with me and he went to get coffee. While I was waiting with my luggage somebody sat down next to me and said, are those your *colones*? That's their currency. I just looked and said no, and while I did that, someone from behind him had grabbed my backpack and run off with it. I yelled and the guy dropped my pack. Within two minutes, security was there.

◆

Analou Sison,
finance manager

I've traveled all over Europe and the only place anyone stuck a gun in my face was in California. My sister and I were robbed. I wanted to tell the guy to take the money. We were having such a good time. Maybe it's an illusion, but Europe feels safe to me.

◆

Mary Works, filmmaker

After the initial shock of the burglary sank in, I remembered how little time had passed between me changing clothes alone in the bus—out of sight of Peter and the others—and the break-in. Whoever the bad guys were, they figured they were stealing from an empty car. But I had been naked and alone in there.

We went to the police station, and the cops were blasé. "This happens all the time, especially to foreigners," the cop who filled out the report told us. Our VW was equipped with California license plates. "Don't expect to get anything back," he said, "Don't expect us to catch them."

Lucky for us, our insurance covered the loss.

Crime is a potential problem in New York and New Delhi, in Austria and Australia. Victims of crimes anywhere often have a difficult time recovering from the emotional impact. But in a foreign country, especially if you are traveling alone, becoming a crime victim can be devastating. The American consulate can help you find counseling if you remain traumatized after a robbery or an attack. Fear can be an immobilizing emotion. It is important for you to reach out for help. You needn't be ashamed if you feel a need to return to familiar and safe surroundings. Going home should always be an alternative.

$\mathcal{T}ips$

➤ If you are a robbery victim and you've followed the advice regarding copying your important papers, you'll be equipped with your credit card numbers, your passport numbers, and all the other crucial information you need to cancel service and obtain replacement cards and documents.

➤ Do not expect the local authorities to respond as the police do at home. Even in societies that seem on the surface to resemble ours, the rules are often quite different. In Mexico, for example, a serious traffic accident often results in both drivers being jailed for the duration of the investigation. Despite the inconvenience, consider doing without your own car and using public transport instead. In addition to eliminating driving stress, riding on buses and trains forces you into ideal opportunities for meeting the locals.

➤ If you become involved with a foreign criminal justice system—either as a victim of a crime or under suspicion of committing a crime—make every effort to get in touch with the U.S. embassy or closest consulate as soon as possible. The help you can expect varies from country to country, and depends on the specific government personnel you encounter. At the very least, you can probably count on them to con-tact your friends and relatives back home. Under emergency conditions, the U.S. government may advance you enough money to return home.

I've been mugged once and ironically it was in a parking lot in California after I got home from six weeks in Asia. My mother was scared for me the whole time I was there and yet I was perfectly safe. I got home and was mugged within a week. I was walking through the parking lot at night and a guy called across to me, "Do you know what time it is?" Of course that's checking to see if you have a watch. I said, "No I don't have a watch on." Then he was in my face and said, "Give me that brooch." We scuffled and he grabbed it. He hit me in the mouth and I ran after him. He went across the freeway and I stopped. I have a scar on my face still to prove it.

◆

Fay Faron,
private detective

➤ The U.S. consulate will not recommend a lawyer if you run afoul of a foreign criminal justice system, but they will provide you with a list of lawyers available to represent you. Consular officers should visit with you periodically if you are held in custody, and should inform your friends and family back home about your status. Do not expect the U.S. government to come to your rescue unless your case is of political value to the current Administration.

➤ The best advice under most circumstances is to try to generate publicity about your predicament if you are facing some sort of criminal prosecution abroad. Most foreign governments do not want to generate worldwide negative publicity about their country and its policies, especially if tourism, as is increasingly the case, is important to their economies.

➤ Within the U.S., your AAA or other automobile club card may be used instead of bail in many jurisdictions. Check with your club for details of what they offer where. Your card also may be valuable at foreign clubs for maps and other services.

One time I was taking a walk in Sofia, Bulgaria in a wonderful park. Some guy was following me and exposing himself. I walked faster and he walked faster. It was one of these wild parks and there weren't very many people around. So I finally got out of the park and went up to a door and knocked. I couldn't speak Bulgarian, but I let them know that I was frightened. The man took off.

◆

Karen Sandel,
international consultant

It was probably around 7:30 when I left the Paris apartment. When the train arrived, I foolishly got into a car that was otherwise unoccupied. I heard the door to the compartment behind me open. I was sitting there when suddenly someone grabbed my breast from behind. Rage, I tell you, absolute rage filled my heart, and I jumped up to face a young man about my size. I immediately positioned myself in the most basic self-defense pose—a semi-crouch with both hands positioned in front of me—and I yelled NOOO!! as loud as I possibly could right in his face.

This startled him for a moment and he backed up. At that moment some more people came into our car, and he sat down in the back of the car. I moved into the next car. When we got to my stop, I exited the train, and so did he. It was very crowded, and he didn't try to approach me. But he made some lewd faces and some general French gutter talk followed, as we went our separate ways.

♦

Jenny Teaford, publicist

Chapter Fourteen

USING THE INTERNET

I daresay that being alone in Yokohama for you is equivalent to negotiating
passage through the Chicago Airport for me.

—*Letter from Flannery O'Connor to Maryat Lee (17 April 1957)*

———

I always call myself a Luddite. I'm certainly a late adapter
to technology. Give me a fountain pen and paper over a
computer any old day, I'm fast to say. But in reality,
especially as a traveler, the internet is a tool I now use routine-
ly. I find cheap airfares and car rentals on the net, I choose
hotels online. But most important, I'm able to research details
about my destinations in minutes from my kitchen table. If, for
some reason, you still are not internet literate, become so today.
Because once you're off on your next trip, you'll find it indis-
pensable for staying in touch.

Most resources we refer to in this book, from the Centers to
Disease Control to the American Automobile Association, offer
their services online. You can obtain answers to most routine
pre-departure questions without leaving home. U.S. State
Department travel warnings are posted in detail on its site,
including esoteric details such as "It is illegal in Laos to invite
Lao nationals of the opposite sex to one's hotel room," and
"Foreigners in Saudi Arabia have been arrested in the past for
'improper dress.'"

A quick internet search using key words such as "women"
along with "travel" and "safe" while we were finishing this book
provided a deluge of information.

An article by Canadian writer Dawn McCoy-Ullrich reminded me that some hotels are developing services specifically tailored for women business travelers, services that women traveling for pleasure can make use of and request at hotels that do not yet offer them. Examples include so-called networking tables at the hotel restaurants so women can eat with other solo women travelers instead of alone, phone calls to the room five minutes before a laundry or meal delivery to insure that the guest is properly attired, and escorts for joggers.

"Security became quite an issue for me during a recent stay at a large hotel," writes McCoy-Ullrich. "As I entered the hotel from the parkade, a man carrying a mop was getting on the empty elevator. He held the door for me. Feeling somewhat rude, but concerned about my personal safety, I politely declined to ride with him. As the elevator door closed, he shook his head." She says she doesn't regret her caution. "Although some may think I was being overly cautious, the reality is that in this day and age, women have to take extra precautions to stay out of vulnerable situations that could lead to physical or emotional harm."

As many times as I've traveled, I always go into regret-mode up to a week before the trip. I wish that I hadn't committed to the travel plans and could just stay home. It seems like too much trouble to get ready and I anticipate all the unknowns and uncertainties ahead. However, I've never acted on these feelings and cancelled a trip. I have never regretted traveling—ever. Quite the opposite.

◆

Monica Kamsvaag,
graphic artist

The magic of the internet means there is no need to limit yourself to hometown sources. You're just a click away, for example, from the Australian government's Department of Foreign Affairs and Trade site. There you'll find a page dedicated to women travelers with suggestions from another perspective.

"Hitchhiking is extremely risky," say the Aussies, "there are very few, if any, places left in the world where hitchhiking is safe for women." They agree with McCoy-Ullrich to watch out in elevators. "Be wary of being alone in lifts as some thieves 'work' high-rise buildings waiting for victims." They add trains to the worry list. "Don't get into train carriage compartments where you would be the only passenger, or stay in one alone if everyone else gets off—attackers are known to target women alone in trains." And they point out that your routine at home can get you in trouble abroad. "In some countries, medications which may be readily available in Australia are illegal. If in doubt, check with the Australian consulates or embassies of the countries you intend to visit to ensure that your medicines, and the quantities you will be carrying, are legal."

The online magazine *Salon* weighs in with an article specific to women interested in traveling alone to Cambodia (not a great idea is the conclusion). If you like groups, check out Women Traveling Together. From their web site you can arrange a group trip with all-female companions. Journeywoman.com helps women travelers connect with other women once they're already on the road, and offers advice about specific destinations from a woman's point of view.

In the U.S., 50 percent of business travelers are now women, and the majority of them travel alone. The numbers are similar in Britain, prompting the BBC to post this on its site: "Often the risks you face overseas are the same kind of risks you face even in your hometown, and a little common sense can be all that's needed for safe traveling." Ask, recommends the BBC. "Listen to other people. Asking other people about their experiences may save you from having to make all those mistakes yourself."

An Illinois travel agency called Egypt Tours & Travel posts a page on its site designed to debunk the worries of women who fear traveling to the Middle East and to Moslem countries, especially alone. "Certainly, there are countries that actually are unsafe for Americans to visit under the current political climate," notes the company, "such as Iraq, Sudan, and Algeria. But other Middle Eastern countries, such as Egypt, Jordan, and Syria are completely safe, as well as

Traveling takes me away from the ordinary so I can involve myself in mystery. It gives me a chance to meet the unknown in myself and others. I love experiencing new and different through old and ancient. I become more tolerant of differences in people at home when I travel. I speak less and listen more. I become braver.

♦

Janelle Va Melvin,
hospice chaplain

extraordinary tourist destinations. If you would like to travel to a country like Egypt, Jordan, or Syria, don't cancel your travel plans because of Iraq or Sudan. The Middle East is about one and a half times larger geographically than the United States. Countries in the Middle East are spread far apart, and although there are problems in some of them, much of the region is, in fact, very safe. Many clients say, 'I worry about what's happening in Israel.' Here's a similar situation: If you live in Cleveland, Ohio and you want to fly to Houston, Texas, and an earthquake happens in San Francisco on the day you planned to fly, would you cancel your plans to go to Houston? No! Because you are familiar with the United States, you would realize that the earthquake wouldn't affect or interfere with your trip at all!"

Come to Egypt, encourages Egypt Tours & Travel. And its site includes this exchange of questions and answers to try to put women at ease.

Q: Is it safe for a single woman to travel to the Middle East without a man companion or a husband and how would I be perceived?

A: Yes, of course it is safe, and you would not stand out being alone. In addition, our staff is there to cater to your safety and comfort. Also more than 55 percent of Egypt Tours & Travel clients are women traveling alone.

Q: (Women ask:) Do I have to cover myself or my head? I want to respect the culture and I do not want to offend anyone when I get there.

A: Americans see the covered women of Saudi Arabia, Kuwait, Yemen, and Iran and think that in all Middle Eastern countries women are required to cover themselves. This is not really true. For example, in Egypt more than 60 percent of the Egyptian women are not veiled. Even among those that do wear veils, most wear just the head-cover and not the full body veil.

Q: It seems that in the Middle East, the culture is so conservative. I wonder if I'll even feel comfortable wearing shorts?

A: Many Middle Eastern cultures are much more open and liberal than most Americans assume or think. Did you know that women in Syria and Lebanon serve in the military and police force? In Egypt, women work, smoke, drink alcohol, go to clubs and discos, wear shorts, tight jeans, and miniskirts, etc. In fact, in these countries you may also come across some strip clubs and topless bars. In Egypt, there are topless beaches at some of the Red Sea resorts. Of course, this is not to say what you should or should not wear in the Middle East, but it should show you that American tourists can wear shorts in Egypt, Jordan, Syria, etc., without having a problem and without offending the locals."

A site called Pagewise offers a reminder that danger can lurk around the corner when we get home. "When traveling close to home, do not get overconfident. Crime can happen even when we are traveling close to home." The U.S. government Citizen Information Center site offers a booklet for a dollar titled "Tips for Women Traveling Alone." The Canadian government's Department of Foreign Affairs and International Trade site offers its version, called "Her Own Way: Advice for the Woman Traveller."

"Surf the net," advise the Canadians. "Post your queries on online bulletin boards. You could get responses from helpful travelers around the world. But beware of those who may be using the net for unsavory purposes." The Canadian book, available online as a pdf, is jammed with specific information for women, such as, "In Southeast Asia, signs are posted at religious landmarks asking women not to enter if they're menstruating."

I do not burden myself by traveling with my laptop anymore. The world is packed with internet cafés. In the developing world, these access points are often wonderfully inexpensive, fifty cents or a dollar an hour is not an uncommon price. In the First World, use of a public machine can be dear: Kinkos charges at least twenty cents a minute, and more in some cities. But there are First World bargains, too, especially at internet cafés in working-class neighborhoods. Around the corner from my lodgings in Barcelona, I could stay online for one hour for a euro. Phone calls from internet cafés and phone shops are often absurdly cheap, too, and usually much less expensive than using a public phone box. Some hotels offer inexpensive internet access, and some offer the service for no charge.

But be careful. Resist the temptation to leash yourself to home. It's easy to spend hours in front of the screen, emailing back and forth to friends and lovers, work and school, while the real world you left home to experience passes you by outside the internet café's window. Of course pick a hometown contact to say in touch with, someone who knows where you are and will send out the alert if you fail to check in at previously agreed times. The internet is an important new safety and security arrow for women traveling, but it's crucial to remember when to leave it in your quiver.

Tips

➤ It's worthwhile to check the Homeland Security Department's Transportation Security Administration web site periodically prior to and during travel. This official U.S. government site assesses safety and security for travelers from the U.S government perspective. Perhaps more important, it offers a guide to the rules and regulations travelers in the U.S. face in the post-9/11 world. See www.tsa.gov/public.

➤ Seek non-U.S.-based sources on the internet to provide you with advice and information that may be at odds with the official U.S. government line. Such information and advice may also reinforce what U.S. sources recommend and thus help you with your decisions about destinations and routes. Most nations with an English-speaking population offer government web sites filled with travel advisories.

➤ Using a basic search engine such as Google will reap a wealth of information regarding the security of your route and destination. If, for example, you enter "Nepal safety travel," you'll find more than 200,000 internet hits advising travelers to be wary of everything from altitude sickness to violent political activities. As always, make sure that you're paying attention to credible internet sources, and seek at least two such sources for critical information.

➤ The travelers' grapevine has always been a key source of close-to-the-ground information on travel conditions. In the old days this meant meeting travelers at cafés, restaurants, or hotels and swapping stories. Today you can also get this kind of information online, and sometimes it's more useful than what's being reported by governments or the press. Two good sites are Lonely Planet's Thorn Tree (thorntree.lonelyplanet.com) and Bootsnall.com's Discussion Boards (boards.bootsnall.com/2/OpenTopic).

➤ Many guidebook publishers offer updates to their books on their web sites. Taking the time to check these sources before you leave and from internet cafés en route is a terrific device for keeping current with changing safety and security issues on the road. Good sites include www.lonelyplanet.com, www.roughguides.com, http://www.ricksteves.com, and—of course—www.travelerstales.com.

RISK AND REWARD

What, after all, is adventure but
inconvenience properly regarded?

—G.K. Chesterton

———

*S*afety and security mean taking care of yourself in all ways. You want to feel as good about yourself on the road as you do at home. After all, it's your trip.

I'm not a paranoid traveler, and most of the situations we point out in this book won't happen to you. I've traveled all over the world, from the wilderness to the cities, alone and with others. My overall experiences and memories are spectacular.

For his work as a news reporter, Peter travels to some of the most dangerous places and situations in the world, and some of the survival tactics he's learned and uses are incorporated into this book because they can be of crucial value for those of us who do not seek out dangerous destinations. I expect the best and usually enjoy the best that traveling offers. But being aware and careful is valuable protection no matter where you go.

Over the years I've traveled, the ideas of safety and security have become so integrated with my routines in my mind that they're automatic—much like locking the door at home. But instinct and awareness always plays the biggest role, and paranoia almost none. To be careful and open is a delicate balance— finding the place where you feel comfortable for whatever level of adventure you want.

Most women have experienced—traveling or at home—a certain vulnerability perceived by almost all cultures as unique to our gender. Even my sons, who know me as a capable, strong, and healthy woman, sometimes act as protectors in situations I have handled alone all my life. Traveling with them as children, I was their protector. As adult men, perhaps they have caught the universal message that many women become victims. Perhaps they consider me too trusting.

Many of my women friends echo my philosophy: intuition and instinct are the best protectors for a woman. Each woman knows her own limits and knows that there is always an element of danger in travel. Risks can be reduced with attention, preparation, and awareness. Knowing dangers and devices for protecting yourself enables you to screen your risks when you can, and reduce or survive them when you can't.

May you have a wonderful and carefree trip.

RESOURCES AND REFERENCES

Books, Magazines, and Newsletters

A few books about women traveling to consider while on the road, or before you leave.

Anthologies and Travelogues

Alpine, Lisa, et al., eds. *Wild Writing Women: Stories of World Travel.* Guilford, Conn.: Globe Pequot, 2002. The WWW—a gathering of twelve women—travel the globe, returning as often as they can to share life's adventures, expressed here with sensitivity and verve.

Bond, Marybeth, ed. *A Woman's World.* San Francisco: Travelers' Tales, 2003. Awarded the Lowell Thomas Gold Medal Award from the Society of American Travel Writers for Best Travel Book. An eloquent collection of women's stories that will move you out of your armchair and take you along paths lined with memory, the spirit of adventure, and the strength of womanhood.

Bond, Marybeth, ed. *A Woman's Europe.* San Francisco: Travelers' Tales, 2004. An exhilarating collection of inspirational, adventurous, and entertaining stories of women exploring the sites—both famous and little-known—of America's favorite continent: Europe.

Griest, Stephanie Elizondo. *Around the Bloc: My Life in Moscow, Beijing, and Havana.* New York: Villard, 2004. A woman's experiences in the Communist world.

Jansz, Natania and Miranda Davies, eds. *More Women Travel: Adventures and Advice from More Than 60 Countries.* London: Rough Guides, 1995. Anthology with useful notes at the end of each tale, offering a listing of special problems women may encounter in the country where the story took place.

Jansz, Natania and Miranda Davies, eds. *Women Travel: A Rough Guide Special* (4th ed.). London: Rough Guides, 1999. An anthology of journeys, spanning some 60 countries and highlighting the pleasures and pitfalls of travel, including particular concerns faced in adjusting to different customs and cultures.

Laqueur, Walter, ed. *The Terrorism Reader: A Historical Anthology.* New Jersey: New American Library. A unique anthology that brings together the most notable proponents, critics, and analysts of terrorism from ancient times to today.

Laufer, Peter. *Nightmare Abroad: Stories of Americans Imprisoned in Foreign Lands.* San Francisco: Mercury House, 1993. The result of research that took Peter around the world to dozens of countries where he learned about the plight of Americans in jails, many of whom are women.

Lee, Elaine, ed. *Go Girl!: The Black Woman's Book of Travel and*

Adventure. Seattle: Eighth Mountain Press, 1997. A collection of fifty-two stories covering the globe, and includes sister-to-sister advice on everything from destinations for a first trip alone to saving money on airfare.

McCauley, Lucy, ed. *Women in the Wild: True Stories of Adventure and Connection*. San Francisco: Travelers' Tales, 2004. A collection of women's travel stories as they explore the natural world.

Morris, Mary and Larry O'Connor, eds. *Maiden Voyages: Writings of Women Travelers*. New York: Vintage Departures, 1993. A collection of stories, old and new, by and for women.

Morris, Mary. *Nothing to Declare: Memoirs of a Woman Traveling Alone*. New York: Houghton Mifflin, 1988. A travelogue and journey into the self as she relates the realities of place, poverty, and machismo of Mexico.

Rogers, Susan Fox. *Going Alone*. Seattle: Seal Press, 2004. This book explores the many ways that women find fulfillment in travel, and is sure to provide ample inspiration for those contemplating their own forays into the wild.

Rogers, Susan Fox, ed. *Solo: On Her Own Adventure*. Seattle: Seal Press, 1996. A collection of twenty-six inspiring stories by women who describe the challenges and exhilarating rewards of going it alone.

Shaffer, Tanya. *Somebody's Heart is Burning: A Woman Wanderer in Africa*. New York: Vintage, 2003. A woman's experiences traveling solo in West Africa.

Simenauer, Jacquelin. *The Single Woman's Travel Guide*. Citadel Press, 2001. This book addresses the issues and problems facing women traveling alone, with helpful resources and tips.

Zepatos, Thalia. *A Journey of One's Own: Uncommon Advice* (3rd ed.). Seattle: Eighth Mountain Press, 2003.This book is packed with information and wisdom for those seeking the less-traveled road.

Advice and Reference Books

Axtel, Roger E., ed. *Do's and Taboos Around the World*. New York: John Wiley & Sons, 1993.

Benjamin, Medea and Miya Rodolfo-Sioson. *The Peace Corps and More: 175 Ways to Work, Study and Travel at Home and Abroad*. Carson, California: Seven Locks Press, Inc., 1997.

Bezruchka, Stephen. *A Passport to Healthy Travel* (3rd ed.). Seattle: Mountaineers Books, 1999.

Bond, Marybeth. *Gutsy Mamas: Travel Tips and Wisdom for Mothers on the Road*. San Francisco: Travelers' Tales, 1998. Indispensible pocket guide full of tips and roadworthy wisdom.

Bond, Marybeth. *Gusty Women: Travel Tips and Wisdom for the Road* (2nd ed.). San Francisco: Travelers' Tales, 2001. Contains funny, instructive, inspiring travel vignettes and tips for novice and experienced travelers.

Brewer, James D. *The Danger from Strangers: Confronting the Threat of Assault*. New York: Plenum Press, 1994.

Brownmiller, Susan. *Against Our Will*. New York: Ballantine, 1993. The classic on rape that can help women prepare to guard against sexual assault on the road.

Buchwald, Emilie, Pamela Fletcher, and Martha Roth, eds. *Transforming a Rape Culture*. Minneapolis: Milkweed Editions, 2004. An anthology of articles on rape.

Cummings, Stephen M.D. and Dana Ullman, M.P.H. *Everybody's Guide to Homeopathic Medicines* (2nd ed). New York: Jeremy P. Tarcher/Putnam Books, 1991.

de Becker, Gavin. *The Gift of Fear*. New York: Dell, 1998. Compendium of priceless ideas and experiences directing women to understand and recognize their natural instincts for danger.

Devine, Elizabeth and Nancy L. Braganti. *The Travelers' Guide to Asian Customs and Manners*. New York: St. Martin's Press, 1986.

Devine, Elizabeth and Nancy L. Braganti. *The Travelers' Guide to Latin American Customs and Manners*. New York: St. Martin's Press, 2000.

McMillon, Bill. *Volunteer Vacations: Short Term Adventures That Will Benefit You and Others* (8th ed.). Chicago: Chicago Review Press, 2003.

Moss, Maggie and Gemma Moss. *Handbook for Women Travellers*. London: Platkus Books, 1995. Collection of tips along with tales of woe and successful traveling from over 100 of their friends.

Panos, Maesimund B. M.D. and Jane Heimlich. *Homeopathic Medicine at Home.* New York: J.P. Tarcher, 1981.

Pelton, Robert Young, Coskun Aral, and Wink Dulles. *The World's Most Dangerous Places* (4th ed.). New York: Harper Resource, 2000.

Schroeder, Dirk. *Staying Healthy in Asia, Africa, and Latin America* (5th ed.). New York: Avalon Travel Publishing, 2000.

Sterling, Richard. *The Fearless Diner: Travel Tips and Wisdom for Eating Around the World.* San Francisco: Travelers' Tales., 1997. A pocket primer on world gastronomy which incorporates essay, anecdote, and voices of experience to guide the reader through the realm of adventure eating.

Strong, Sanford. *Strong on Defense: Survival Rules to Protect You and Your Family from Crime.* New York: Simon & Schuster, Inc., 1996. Valuable techniques and precautions that can be used to protect yourself in any situation.

Survival. Department of the Army field manual available in government book stores. Offers practical advice for far-flung adventurers and step-by-step procedures for navigating, finding water, even slaughtering and preparing wildlife.

Warshaw, Robin. *I Never Called it Rape.* New York: HarperPerennial, 1994. The Ms. magazine report on recognizing, fighting, and surviving date and acquaintance rape.

Wiseman, John. *The SAS Personal Survival Handbook.* London: HarperCollins UK, 2000.

Wilson-Howarth, Jane. *Shitting Pretty: How to Stay Clean and Healthy While Traveling*. San Francisco: Travelers' Tales, 1999.

Windsor, Natalie. *The Safe Tourist*. Los Angeles: Corkscrew Press, 1995. A collection of useful tips in checklist form.

Travel Newsletters and Magazines

Adventure Women
Adventures worldwide for Women over 30. E-newsletter available.
www.adventurewoman.com

American Woman, Road and Travel
Online magazine with columns on safety and security, automotive, travel arrangements and ideas.
www.roadandtravel.com

Boundless Travel
E-zine
www.boundless-travel.com/newsletters/currentnewsletter.htm

Guava
Independent magazine for women travelers, "always served fresh, to help you get your travel on." Both bi-monthly print, as well as online magazine.
www.guavamag.com

Journeywoman
Women's online travel magazine that inspires women to travel safely and to connect with female travelers internationally.
www.journeywoman.com

Transitions Abroad
Monthly magazine and resource guide to educational and work opportunities abroad.
POB 745
Bennington VT 05201
www.transitionsaborad.com/publications/magazine/

Travel Lady Magazine
Online magazine
www.travellady.com

Services and Organizations

Mail Order Companies

Magellans
Travel-related equipment.
Catalogue: 800-962-4943
www.magellans.com

Orvis
High-end luggage and clothing for travels.
1-888-235-9763
www.orvis.com

Sierra Trading Post
Outlet mall with savings on outdoor apparel and gear.
1-800-713-4534
www.sierratradingpost.com

Travelsmith

In addition to travel-related equipment, Travelsmith offers a
service with live operators with advice on what to bring where,
weather, and other travel-related questions.

Catalogue: 800-950-1600

Travel line: 800-995-7010

www.travelsmith.com

Organizations Specializing in Group and Women's Travel

Above the Clouds Trekking
P.O. Box 388
Hinesburg, VT 05461
800-233-4499

Adventure Associates
P.O. Box 16304
Seattle, WA 98116
206-932-8352

AdventureWomen, Inc.
15033 Kelly Canyon Road
Bozeman, MT 59715
800-804-8686

Austin Lehman Adventures
P.O. Box 81025
Billings, MT 59108
800-575-1540

Backroads
1516 Fifth Street
Berkeley, CA 94710-1740
800-462-2848

Becoming An Outdoorswoman
College of Natural Resources
University of Wisconsin, ST
Stevens Point, WI 54481-3897
877-269-6626

Call of the Wild
2519 Cedar Street
Berkeley, CA 94708
510-849-9292
888-3378-1978 (outside California)

Geographic Expeditions
1008 General Kennedy Avenue
San Francisco, CA 91429
9800-777-9193
www.geoex.com

Inca Floats
1311 63rd Street
Emeryville, CA 94608
510-420-1550

Journeys
4011 Jackson
Ann Arbor, MI 48103
800-255-8735

Mariah Wilderness Expeditions
P.O. Box 248
Point Richmond, CA 94807
415-233-2303

Mountain Travel Sobek
6420 Fairmont Avenue
El Cerrito, CA 94530-3606
800-227-2384

Myths & Mountains
976 Tee Court
Incline Village, NV 89451
800-670-6984

Natural Habitat Adventures
2945 Center Green Court, Suite H
Boulder, CO 80301
800-543-8917

Nature Expeditions International
7860 Peter's Road, Suite F103
Plantation, FL 35824
800-869-0639

Overseas Adventure Travel
625 Mount Auburn Street
Cambridge, MA 02138
800-221-0814

Sheri Griffith Expeditions
P.O. Box 1324

Moab, UT 84532
800-332-2439

Turtle Tours, Inc.
Box 1147/Dept ES
Carefree, AZ 85377
602-488-3688

The Wayfarers
174 Bellevue Avenue
Newport, RI 02840
800-249-4620

Wilderness Travel
801 Allston Way
Berkeley, CA 94710
800-368-2794

Womenship
410 Severn Avenue
The Boathouse
Annapolis, MD 21403
800-342-9295

Women's Travel Club
21401 NE 38th Avenue
Aventura, FL 33180
800-480-4448/305-936-9669

Womentours
Bicycle Tours for Women
P.O. Box 931

Driggs, ID 83422
800-247-1444

Lesbian Travel

Madison Travel (European Travel)
118 Western Road
Hove, East Sussex
BN3 1DB   U.K.
www.madisontravel.com

Ocean Voyager Gay Group Cruise
1275 Bloomfield Avenue, Suite 26A
Fairfield, NJ 07004
973-882-5959
800-435-2531
www.oceanvoyager.com

Olivia Cruises and Resorts
4400 Market Street
Oakland, CA 94608
800-631-6277/510-655-0364

Sacred Journeys for Women
P.O. Box 8007, Roseland Station
Santa Rosa, CA 95407
888-779-6696
www.sacredjourneys.com

Wild Women Expeditions (Canada Travel)
P.O. Box 145, Station B
Sudbury, Ontario

Canada P3E 4N5
705-866-1260
beth@wildwomenexp.com

Travel for the Disabled

Access-Able Travel Source
P.O. Box 1796
Wheat Ridge, CO 80034
303-232-2979
www.access-able.com

Accessible Travel and Leisure
Avionics House, Naas Lane
Gloucester GL2 2SN UK
www.accessibletravel.co.uk

Society for Accessible Travel and Hospitality
347 Fifth Ave., Suite 610
New York, NY 10016
212-447-7284
www.sath.org

House Swaps and Homestays

Australian Homestays and Farmstays
88 Wairarapa Terrace
Mericale, Christchurch
New Zealand
66-3-355-6737
www.australianhomestay.com

British Homestays
24 Temple Avenue.
Shirley, Croyden
London CR0 8QA UK
44-0-208777-3038

Experiment in International Living Federation
P.O. Box 595
Putney, VT 05346
802-387-4210

Friendship Force
57 Forsyth Street NW, Suite 900
Atlanta, GA 30303
404-522-9490

Home Base Holidays
7 Park Avenue
London NI3 5PG UK
44-0-20-8886-8752
www.homebase-hols.com

Home Link International
800-638-3841
www.homelink.org

Intervac Home Exchange
30 Corte San Fernando
Tiburon, A 94920
800-756-HOME
www.intervacus.com

LEX Exchange/LEX America
68 Leonard Street
Belmont, MA 02178
617-489-5800

U.S. Servas
11 John Street, Room 505
New York, NY 10038
212-267-0252

Vacation Exchange Club
P.O. Box 820
Hale'iwa, HI 96712
800-638-3841

Villas & Apartments Abroad, Ltd.
183 Madison Avenue, Suite 281
New York, NY 10016
212-759-1025

Women Welcome Women
c/o Joan Beyette
11215 26th Street SW
Calgary, Alberta T2W 5C6, CANADA

Reference and Research

CDC—Centers for Disease Control
Maintains current specific health warnings filed by region.
888-232-3228
888-232-3299 (phone line to request written information to be
sent via fax)
www.cdc.gov

Homeopathic Educational Services
Mail order house with catalog of homeopathic
books, remedies, travel and home kits
2124 Kittredge St.
Berkeley, CA 94704
510-649-0294
www.homeopathic.com

International Association for Medical Assistance to Travelers
Worldwide directory of English-speaking doctors.
716-754-4883
www.iamat.org

Peters Projection World Map
Friendship Press
P.O. Box 37844
Cincinnati, OH 45222

U.S. State Department
Prepares citizen warnings for particularly dangerous locales.
Recorded announcements of those crisis zones.
202-647-5225
202-647-6201 (to arrange for fax copies of warnings)
Website: http://travel.state.gov

Internet Resources

Search the Internet under "Travel Safety" or "Women, Travel" or
point your browser to the following sites:

Access-Able Travel Source: www.access-able.com

American Woman Road and Travel: www.roadandtravel.com

Bootsnall Ultimate Resource for the Independent Traveler:
www.bootsnall.com

Bureau of Consular Affairs:
www.travel.state.gov/tips_women.html

Centers For Disease Control: www.cdc.gov/travel/travel.html

Embassies and Consulates: www.embassy.org/embassies/

Foreign Commonwealth Office's Travel Advice:
www.fco.gov.uk/travel/default.asp

GoNOMAD – the alternative way to travel:
www.GoNOMAD.com

International Association for Medical Assistance to Travelers:
www.iamat.org

Lonely Planet's Travel Ticker and Postcards:
www.lonelyplanet.com

National Transportation Safety Board: http://www.ntsb.gov

Overseas Security Advisory Council: www.ds-osac.org

Tourism Offices Worldwide Directory: www.towd.com

Transitions Abroad: www.transitionsaborad.com

Travel Health Information Service: www.cdc.gov/travel/

Travel Safety from Safe Within: www.safewithin.com/travelsafe/

The Traveling Woman: www.thetravelingwoman.com

U.S. State Department Travel Warnings & Consular
Information Sheets: http://travel.state.gov/travel_warnings.html

Women's Travel Club: www.womenstravelclub.com

Women Traveling Together: www.women-traveling.com

World Health Organization: www.who.int

World Travel Watch: www.worldtravelwatch.com

Miscellaneous Resources

Credit Card Advice

American Express
U.S.   800-528-4800
Abroad 910-333-321 collect

Diners Club
U.S.   800-346-3779
Abroad 303-790-2433 collect

Discover
U.S.   800-347-2683
Abroad not accepted

Mastercard
U.S.   800-622-7747
Abroad   303-278-8000 collect

Visa
U.S.   800-336-8472
Abroad   410-581-7931 collect

Travelers' Check Advice

American Express
U.S.   800-221-7282
Abroad   offices worldwide

Bank of America
U.S.   800-227-6811
Abroad   410-581-5353 collect

Citicorp
U.S.   800-645-6556
Abroad   813-623-1709 collect

Thomas Cook
U.S.   800-223-7373
Abroad   609-987-7300 collect

Visa
U.S.   800-227-6811/800-732-1322
Abroad   44-173-331-8949 collect

INDEX OF CONTRIBUTORS

About the Authors

Sheila Swan Laufer has been traveling the world for fun and business since the 1960s. From camping in Latin America to luxury resorts in the Old World, from long-distance buses across the American South to first-class airliner seats five miles high, from quaint pensions on the Iberian Peninsula to five-star hotels in Oceana, she has experienced the extremes travel offers—taking notes all along the way.

Peter Laufer is an award-winning journalist whose career has taken him to many of the world's most dangerous destinations. While researching his book *Nightmare Abroad*, he traveled around the world, stopping in twenty-one countries, interviewing Americans locked up in foreign prisons. Another of his books, *Iron Curtain Rising*, recounts his journey through Eastern Europe during the revolutions of 1989–1990.

Together the two wrote and photographed *Neon Nevada*, a study of the impact of the neon sign on Nevada culture, published by the University of Nevada Press.

NOTES

NOTES

NOTES

NOTES

NOTES

TRAVELERS' TALES
THE POWER OF A GOOD STORY

New Releases

THE BEST TRAVELERS' TALES 2004　　　　$16.95
True Stories from Around the World
Edited by James O'Reilly, Larry Habegger & Sean O'Reilly
The launch of a new annual collection presenting fresh, lively storytelling and compelling narrative to make the reader laugh, weep, and buy a plane ticket.

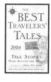

INDIA　　　　$18.95
True Stories
Edited by James O'Reilly & Larry Habegger
"*Travelers' Tales India* is ravishing in the texture and variety of tales."
　　　　　　　　　　—*Foreign Service Journal*

A WOMAN'S EUROPE　　　　$17.95
True Stories
Edited by Marybeth Bond
An exhilarating collection of inspirational, adventurous, and entertaining stories by women exploring the romantic continent of Europe. From the bestselling author Marybeth Bond.

WOMEN IN THE WILD　　　　$17.95
True Stories of Adventure and Connection
Edited by Lucy McCauley
"A spiritual, moving, and totally female book to take you around the world and back."　　　　　　　　　　—*Mademoiselle*

CHINA　　　　$18.95
True Stories
Edited by James O'Reilly, Larry Habegger & Sean O'Reilly
A must for any traveler to China, for anyone wanting to learn more about the Middle Kingdom, offering a breadth and depth of experience from both new and well-known authors; helps make the China experience unforgettable and transforming.

BRAZIL　　　　$17.95
True Stories
Edited by Annette Haddad & Scott Doggett
Introduction by Alex Shoumatoff
"Only the lowest wattage dim bulb would visit Brazil without reading this book."　　　　　　　—Tim Cahill, author of *Pass the Butterworms*

THE PENNY PINCHER'S PASSPORT TO LUXURY TRAVEL (2ND EDITION)　　　　$14.95
The Art of Cultivating Preferred Customer Status
By Joel L. Widzer
Completely updated and revised, this 2nd edition of the popular guide to traveling like the rich and famous without being either describes, both philosophically and in practical terms, how to obtain luxurious travel benefits by building relationships with airlines and other travel companies.

Women's Travel

A WOMAN'S EUROPE $17.95
True Stories
Edited by Marybeth Bond
An exhilarating collection of inspirational, adventurous, and entertaining stories by women exploring the romantic continent of Europe. From the bestselling author Marybeth Bond.

WOMEN IN THE WILD $17.95
True Stories of Adventure and Connection
Edited by Lucy McCauley
"A spiritual, moving, and totally female book to take you around the world and back."
— *Mademoiselle*

A WOMAN'S WORLD $18.95
True Stories of Life on the Road
Edited by Marybeth Bond
Introduction by Dervla Murphy

— ★ ★ ★ —

Lowell Thomas Award
—Best Travel Book

A MOTHER'S WORLD $14.95
Journeys of the Heart
Edited by Marybeth Bond & Pamela Michael
"These stories remind us that motherhood is one of the great unifying forces in the world."
— *San Francisco Examiner*

A WOMAN'S PASSION FOR TRAVEL $17.95
More True Stories from A Woman's World
Edited by Marybeth Bond & Pamela Michael
"A diverse and gripping series of stories!"
— Arlene Blum, author of
Annapurna: A Woman's Place

Food

ADVENTURES IN WINE $17.95
True Stories of Vineyards and Vintages around the World
Edited by Thom Elkjer
Humanity, community, and brotherhood comprise the marvelous virtues of the wine world. This collection toasts the warmth and wonders of this large extended family in stories by travelers who are wine novices and experts alike.

FOOD $18.95
A Taste of the Road
Edited by Richard Sterling
Introduction by Margo True

— ★ ★ ★ —

Silver Medal Winner of the
Lowell Thomas Award
—Best Travel Book

HER FORK IN THE ROAD $16.95
Women Celebrate Food and Travel
Edited by Lisa Bach
A savory sampling of stories by the best writers in and out of the food and travel fields.

THE ADVENTURE OF FOOD $17.95
True Stories of Eating Everything
Edited by Richard Sterling
"Bound to whet appetites for more than food." — *Publishers Weekly*

THE FEARLESS DINER $7.95
Travel Tips and Wisdom for Eating around the World
By Richard Sterling
Combines practical advice on foodstuffs, habits, and etiquette, with hilarious accounts of others' eating adventures.

Travel Humor

SAND IN MY BRA AND OTHER MISADVENTURES $14.95
Funny Women Write from the Road
Edited by Jennifer L. Leo
"A collection of ridiculous and sublime travel experiences."
—*San Francisco Chronicle*

HYENAS LAUGHED AT ME $14.95 AND NOW I KNOW WHY
The Best of Travel Humor and Misadventure
Edited by Sean O'Reilly, Larry Habegger, and James O'Reilly
Hilarious, outrageous and reluctant voyagers indulge us with the best misadventures around the world.

LAST TROUT IN VENICE $14.95
The Far-Flung Escapades of an Accidental Adventurer
By Doug Lansky
"Traveling with Doug Lansky might result in a considerably shortened life expectancy...but what a way to go."
—Tony Wheeler, Lonely Planet Publications

NOT SO FUNNY WHEN IT HAPPENED $12.95
The Best of Travel Humor and Misadventure
Edited by Tim Cahill
Laugh with Bill Bryson, Dave Barry, Anne Lamott, Adair Lara, and many more.

THERE'S NO TOILET PAPER...ON THE ROAD LESS TRAVELED $12.95
The Best of Travel Humor and Misadventure
Edited by Doug Lansky

— ★ ★ ★ —
Humor Book of the Year
—Independent Publisher's Book Award

— ★ ★ ★ —
ForeWord Gold Medal Winner—Humor Book of the Year

Travelers' Tales Classics

COAST TO COAST $16.95
A Journey Across 1950s America
By Jan Morris
After reporting on the first Everest ascent in 1953, Morris spent a year journeying across the United States. In brilliant prose, Morris records with exuberance and curiosity a time of innocence in the U.S.

TRADER HORN $16.95
A Young Man's Astounding Adventures in 19th Century Equatorial Africa
By Alfred Aloysius Horn
Here is the stuff of legends—thrills and danger, wild beasts, serpents, and savages. An unforgettable and vivid portrait of a vanished Africa.

THE ROYAL ROAD TO ROMANCE $14.95
By Richard Halliburton
"Laughing at hardships, dreaming of beauty, ardent for adventure, Halliburton has managed to sing into the pages of this glorious book his own exultant spirit of youth and freedom."
—*Chicago Post*

UNBEATEN TRACKS IN JAPAN $14.95
By Isabella L. Bird
Isabella Bird was one of the most adventurous women travelers of the 19th century with journeys to Tibet, Canada, Korea, Turkey, Hawaii, and Japan. A fascinating read.

THE RIVERS RAN EAST $16.95
By Leonard Clark
Clark is the original Indiana Jones, telling the breathtaking story of his search for the legendary El Dorado gold in the Amazon.

Spiritual Travel

THE SPIRITUAL GIFTS OF TRAVEL $16.95
The Best of Travelers' Tales
Edited by James O'Reilly and Sean O'Reilly
Favorite stories of transformation on the road
that shows the myriad ways travel indelibly
alters our inner landscapes.

PILGRIMAGE $16.95
Adventures of the Spirit
Edited by Sean O'Reilly & James O'Reilly
Introduction by Phil Cousineau

— ★ ★ ★ —

ForeWord Silver Medal Winner
— Travel Book of the Year

THE ROAD WITHIN $18.95
True Stories of Transformation
and the Soul
Edited by Sean O'Reilly, James O'Reilly &
Tim O'Reilly

— ★ ★ ★ —

Independent Publisher's Book Award
—Best Travel Book

THE WAY OF THE WANDERER $14.95
Discover Your True Self Through Travel
By David Yeadon
Experience transformation through travel
with this delightful, illustrated collection by
award-winning author David Yeadon.

A WOMAN'S PATH $16.95
Women's Best Spiritual Travel Writing
Edited by Lucy McCauley, Amy G. Carlson &
Jennifer Leo
"A sensitive exploration of women's lives that
have been unexpectedly and spiritually
touched by travel experiences.... Highly
recommended."
—Library Journal

THE ULTIMATE JOURNEY $17.95
Inspiring Stories of Living and Dying
James O'Reilly, Sean O'Reilly & Richard
Sterling
"A glorious collection of writings about the
ultimate adventure. A book to keep by one's
bedside—and close to one's heart."
—Philip Zaleski, editor,
The Best Spiritual Writing series

Special Interest

THE BEST TRAVELERS' TALES 2004 $16.95
True Stories from Around the World
Edited by James O'Reilly, Larry Habegger &
Sean O'Reilly
The launch of a new annual collection pre-
senting fresh, lively storytelling and compelling
narrative to make the reader laugh, weep, and
buy a plane ticket.

TESTOSTERONE PLANET $17.95
True Stories from a Man's World
Edited by Sean O'Reilly, Larry Habegger &
James O'Reilly
Thrills and laughter with some of today's best
writers: Sebastian Junger, Tim Cahill, Bill
Bryson, and Jon Krakauer.

THE GIFT OF TRAVEL $14.95
The Best of Travelers' Tales
Edited by Larry Habegger, James O'Reilly
& Sean O'Reilly
"Like gourmet chefs in a French market, the
editors of Travelers' Tales pick, sift, and prod
their way through the weighty shelves of con-
temporary travel writing, creaming off the
very best."
—William Dalrymple, author of City of Djinns

DANGER! $17.95
True Stories of Trouble and Survival
Edited by James O'Reilly, Larry Habegger &
Sean O'Reilly
"Exciting...for those who enjoy living on the
edge or prefer to read the survival stories of
others, this is a good pick."
—Library Journal

365 TRAVEL $14.95
A Daily Book of Journeys, Meditations, and Adventures
Edited by Lisa Bach
An illuminating collection of travel wisdom and adventures that reminds us all of the lessons we learn while on the road.

THE GIFT OF RIVERS $14.95
True Stories of Life on the Water
Edited by Pamela Michael
Introduction by Robert Hass
...a soulful compendium of wonderful stories that illuminate, educate, inspire, and delight."
—David Brower,
Chairman of Earth Island Institute

FAMILY TRAVEL $17.95
The Farther You Go, the Closer You Get
Edited by Laura Manske
"This is family travel at its finest."
—*Working Mother*

LOVE & ROMANCE $17.95
True Stories of Passion on the Road
Edited by Judith Babcock Wylie
"A wonderful book to read by a crackling fire." —*Romantic Traveling*

THE GIFT OF BIRDS $17.95
True Encounters with Avian Spirits
Edited by Larry Habegger & Amy G. Carlson
"These are all wonderful, entertaining stories offering a *bird's-eye view!* of our avian friends."
—*Booklist*

A DOG'S WORLD $12.95
True Stories of Man's Best Friend on the Road
Edited by Christine Hunsicker
Introduction by Maria Goodavage

Travel Advice

THE PENNY PINCHER'S PASSPORT TO LUXURY TRAVEL $14.95
(2ND EDITION)
The Art of Cultivating Preferred Customer Status
By Joel L. Widzer
Completely updated and revised, this 2nd edition of the popular guide to traveling like the rich and famous without being either describes, both philosophically and in practical terms, how to obtain luxurious travel benefits by building relationships with airlines and other travel companies.

SAFETY AND SECURITY $12.95
FOR WOMEN WHO TRAVEL
By Sheila Swan & Peter Laufer
"An engaging book, with plenty of first-person stories about strategies women have used while traveling to feel safe but still find their way into a culture."
—*Chicago Herald*

THE FEARLESS SHOPPER $14.95
How to Get the Best Deals on the Planet
By Kathy Borrus
"Anyone who reads *The Fearless Shopper* will come away a smarter, more responsible shopper and a more curious, culturally attuned traveler."
—Jo Mancuso, *The Shopologist*

SHITTING PRETTY $12.95
How to Stay Clean and Healthy While Traveling
By Dr. Jane Wilson-Howarth
A light-hearted book about a serious subject for millions of travelers—staying healthy on the road—written by international health expert, Dr. Jane Wilson-Howarth.

GUTSY WOMEN $12.95
More Travel Tips and Wisdom for the Road
By Marybeth Bond
Second Edition
Packed with funny, instructive, and inspiring advice for women heading out to see the world.

GUTSY MAMAS $7.95
Travel Tips and Wisdom for Mothers on the Road
By Marybeth Bond
A delightful guide for mothers traveling with their children—or without them!

Destination Titles

ALASKA $18.95
Edited by Bill Sherwonit, Andromeda Romano-Lax, & Ellen Bielawski

AMERICA $19.95
Edited by Fred Setterberg

AMERICAN SOUTHWEST $17.95
Edited by Sean O'Reilly & James O'Reilly

AUSTRALIA $17.95
Edited by Larry Habegger

BRAZIL $17.95
Edited by Annette Haddad & Scott Doggett
Introduction by Alex Shoumatoff

CENTRAL AMERICA $17.95
Edited by Larry Habegger & Natanya Pearlman

CHINA $18.95
Edited by James O'Reilly, Larry Habegger & Sean O'Reilly

CUBA $17.95
Edited by Tom Miller

FRANCE $18.95
Edited by James O'Reilly, Larry Habegger & Sean O'Reilly

GRAND CANYON $17.95
Edited by Sean O'Reilly, James O'Reilly & Larry Habegger

GREECE $18.95
Edited by Larry Habegger, Sean O'Reilly & Brian Alexander

HAWAI'I $17.95
Edited by Rick & Marcie Carroll

HONG KONG $17.95
Edited by James O'Reilly, Larry Habegger & Sean O'Reilly

INDIA $18.95
Edited by James O'Reilly & Larry Habegger

IRELAND $18.95
Edited by James O'Reilly, Larry Habegger & Sean O'Reilly

ITALY $18.95
Edited by Anne Calcagno
Introduction by Jan Morris

JAPAN $17.95
Edited by Donald W. George & Amy G. Carlson

MEXICO $17.95
Edited by James O'Reilly & Larry Habegger

NEPAL $17.95
Edited by Rajendra S. Khadka

PARIS $18.95
Edited by James O'Reilly, Larry Habegger & Sean O'Reilly

PROVENCE $16.95
Edited by James O'Reilly & Tara Austen Weaver

SAN FRANCISCO $18.95
Edited by James O'Reilly, Larry Habegger & Sean O'Reilly

SPAIN $19.95
Edited by Lucy McCauley

THAILAND $18.95
Edited by James O'Reilly & Larry Habegger

TIBET $18.95
Edited by James O'Reilly & Larry Habegger

TURKEY $18.95
Edited by James Villers Jr.

TUSCANY $16.95
Edited by James O'Reilly & Tara Austen Weaver
Introduction by Anne Calcagno

Footsteps Series

THE FIRE NEVER DIES $14.95
**One Man's Raucous Romp Down the Road of Food,
Passion, and Adventure**
By Richard Sterling
"Sterling's writing is like spitfire, foursquare and jazzy with
crackle...." —*Kirkus Reviews*

ONE YEAR OFF $14.95
**Leaving It All Behind for a Round-the-World Journey
with Our Children**
By David Elliot Cohen
A once-in-a-lifetime adventure generously shared, from the
author/editor of *America 24/7* and *A Day in the Life of Africa*

THE WAY OF THE WANDERER $14.95
Discover Your True Self Through Travel
By David Yeadon
Experience transformation through travel with this delightful,
illustrated collection by award-winning author David Yeadon.

TAKE ME WITH YOU $24.00
A Round-the-World Journey to Invite a Stranger Home
By Brad Newsham
"Newsham is an ideal guide. His journey, at heart, is into
humanity." —Pico Iyer, author of *The Global Soul*

KITE STRINGS OF THE SOUTHERN CROSS $14.95
A Woman's Travel Odyssey
By Laurie Gough
Short-listed for the prestigious Thomas Cook Award, this is an
exquisite rendering of a young woman's search for meaning.

*ForeWord Silver Medal Winner
— Travel Book of the Year*

THE SWORD OF HEAVEN $24.00
A Five Continent Odyssey to Save the World
By Mikkel Aaland
"Few books capture the soul of the road like The *Sword of
Heaven,* a sharp-edged, beautifully rendered memoir that will
inspire anyone."
—Phil Cousineau, author of *The Art of Pilgrimage*

STORM $24.00
**A Motorcycle Journey of Love, Endurance,
and Transformation**
By Allen Noren
"Beautiful, tumultuous, deeply engaging and very satisfying.
Anyone who looks for truth in travel will find it here."
—Ted Simon, author of *Jupiter's Travels*

*ForeWord Gold Medal Winner
— Travel Book of the Year*